DIGITAL
CURRENCIES

DIGITAL
CURRENCIES

UNLOCKING THE SECRETS OF CRYPTO-CURRENCIES

DAVID PETERSON

PARTRIDGE

To order additional copies of this book, contact
Toll Free 800 101 2657 (Singapore)
Toll Free 1 800 81 7340 (Malaysia)
orders.singapore@partridgepublishing.com

www.partridgepublishing.com/singapore

DISCLAIMER NOTICE

The information included in this book is for educational purposes only and is not meant to be a substitute for seeking the advice of a professional. The author and publisher have made best efforts to ensure the information in this book is accurate. However, they make no warranties as to the accuracy or completeness of the contents herein and cannot be held responsible for any errors, omissions, or dated material.

Liability Disclaimer

By reading this book, you assume all risks associated with using the advice, data and suggestions given below, with a full understanding that you, solely, are responsible for any loss that may occur as a result of putting this information into action in any way, and regardless of your interpretation of the advice.

WHAT YOU'LL FIND IN THIS BOOK?

"The Digital Revolution is marching on and entering every aspect of life." - *Ernst Raue, CEO of ER-GBS Gmbh*

Crypto-currencies aren't without their share of controversies. These virtual currencies have created a revolution in both the economic and the financial front.

Whether the founders of the crypto-currencies such as Satoshi Nakamoto (*Bitcoin*), Charles Lee (*Litecoin*), Paul Snow (*Factom*), Vitalik Buterin (*Ethereum*), and many others have profited from their product is not known.

But their efforts have certainly contributed a digital revolution in the form of a radical new currency – the virtual currency - that once all the loopholes are plugged can one day replace the paper and plastic currencies as they had replaced gold as a mode of payment in the past.

The introduction of the digital currencies has brought forth a whole new set of regulations, technical jargons, and standard practices. In the eBook, *Digital Currencies - Unlocking the Secrets of the Crypto-Currencies*, you will uncover the secrets of the virtual currency including:

- History and evolution of crypto-currency,

- The next generation of digital currencies,

- Technology that powers the digital currency,

- Big data and the network effect,

- The market equilibrium and the baseline mode,

- Legal and tax issues regarding virtual currency, and

- much more.

So, are you ready to get in-depth knowledge about the crypto-currency revolution? Let's delve in to find out more.

TABLE OF CONTENTS

SECTION I
Bitcoin and The Alternative Cryptocurrencies

SECTION II
BIG DATA AND NETWORK EFFECT

SECTION III

FINANCE MARKETS AND BITCOIN REGULATION & TAXATION

SECTION IV

FINANCIAL INNOVATION AND INTERNET OF MONEY

SECTION I

BITCOIN AND THE ALTERNATIVE CRYPTOCURRENCIES

CHAPTER ONE

INTRODUCTION TO DIGITAL CURRENCIES

Digital currencies such as Bitcoin, Litecoin, and others represent the latest evolution of money and payments. A digital currency in its most basic form is a decentralized and peer-to-peer medium of exchange that represents the latest evolution of currencies.

Similar to paper currencies, digital currencies are designed for the exchange of goods between two or more individuals.

Since the virtual currency makes use of the principles of cryptography to secure the payments and control the creation of new coins, it is also known by the name of crypto-currency.

1.1   The Next Generation of Money and Payments

The first crypto-currency was the 'Bitcoin' that was introduced in 2009 by a software developer named Satoshi Nakamoto. The main idea behind the creation of the virtual currency was a mode of payment that was self-regulating, transferred electronically, and involved very low financial charges.

The introduction of bitcoins heralded the beginning of the next generation of currencies that despite being in their infant stages are gaining worldwide popularity.

An individual that wants to use a crypto-currency must:

- Obtain a digital wallet for storing the crypto-currency

- Create a unique public address for the digital wallet

- Use the public address to transfer money into and out of the wallet

The public address consists of a string of characters that identify a wallet. Every public address contains a private address that can be used to carry out the transactions. You can think of the address as a personal email address that is used to send digital currencies instead of the emails.

The digital currencies make uses of cryptography in order to create money and validate the transactions. These transactions are appended into a Transaction Blockchain, which is a form of a large public ledger.

Every block in the blockchain consists of the hash value of the previous block and a random number of the next block. The hash value links the previous block with the current one while the random number provides the proof-of-work.

A unique aspect of the crypto-currency is mining. The miners use their computer resource to verify the transaction. Once the transaction has been verified, it becomes a permanent part of the blockchain ledger.

In order to verify a transaction, the miner has to solve a cryptographic puzzle. This puzzle that is known as the proof-of-work scheme was coded in order to prevent the miners from adding a fake transaction and then simply add to the ledger.

The proof-of-work system that we had mentioned earlier is based on a cryptographic hashing algorithm, which is different for different types of crypto-currencies. For the bitcoin, for instance, the fixed size block header is hashed using an algorithm known as SHA-256d. The hashing algorithm for ethereum is dagger hashimoto, while scrypt and ECDSA are the hashing algorithms of litecoin and ripple, respectively.

The economic system of the crypto-currency is based on a group incentive scheme that is crafted in a way that all the users get a fair reward for their efforts in validating the transactions.

A user invests the computer resources to solve the cryptographic puzzle and receive a fair reward in the form of a currency unit that is added to the public blockchain.

Today, people can use crypto-currencies to purchase just about anything that is sold online. Major companies such as Uber, Expedia, Overstock, Zynga, TigerDirect, Fiverr, and many others now allow users to make payments using the digital currency. This is evidence enough of the growing acceptance of crypto-currencies as an alternative currency.

1.2   Digital Currency as an Alternative Currency

Digital currencies are increasingly becoming the new alternative to traditional fiat currency. There are many benefits of the virtual currencies as compared to the paper based currencies that are issued by the central banks of different countries.

Similar to the traditional currencies people can use the currency to buy grocery items, web hosting services, and even cars online.

At the present, digital currency is in its infancy.

While a large number of people have supported the crypto-currency revolution, the masses still use conventional currencies to make the payments.

However, the use of virtual currencies for carrying out the transactions is growing which each passing year

In the month of February 2013, Coinbase that processes bitcoins reported selling about one million dollar worth of bitcoins.[1] In the same year, a company named Internet Archive had announced that it was accepting bitcoins and that it would give salaries to the employees in virtual currency. [2]

Also, in 2013 the University of Nicosia in Cyprus became the first university to allow students to pay fees using the bitcoin.[3]

In the month of December 2014, Microsoft began accepting bitcoin to buy Windows apps and Xbox games.[4] As of 2015, the number of merchants that accepted bitcoin had grown to 160,000.[5]

The Bank of Japan had recognized the virtual currency as a mode of payment in March of 2016 stating that it functions similar to real money.[6] Also, the number of ATMs that use bitcoins as an exchange of payment has doubled over the past year reaching to 770.[7]

While the system is not perfect, the myriad benefits of the payment system over the traditional mode of payment are resulting in increased acceptance of the virtual currency among the masses.

The technology behind the Bitcoin and other crypto-currencies are owned by the individuals. There is no central authority that controls the transaction carried out using the virtual money.

In a way, the crypto-currency perfectly captured the essence of the internet, which is also not controlled by a central authority.

Similar to the World Wide Web, the virtual currency could be used anywhere by anyone at anytime and residing anywhere in the world.

Crypto-currencies including bitcoin are decentralized in that they are not backed by any government. Moreover, the value is not rooted in commodities such as gold or silver.

The supporters of the digital currency say that digital currency is superior to fiat currencies because the values cannot be manipulated by the oligarchs or politicians for profit or politics.

The integrity of the digital currency is guaranteed by mathematical rules. The power of the virtual currencies rests in the open source and distributed networks.

Global investors who are troubled by the cycle of credit and financial busts can look to digital currency as a mode of exchange of funds. It's is dubbed by some experts as Gold 2.0.

Similar to the precious metals, the supply of crypto-currencies is limited. However, the scarcity of the virtual currencies is algorithmic instead of natural.

Virtual currencies are created only when they are 'mined'. Miners invest their state of the art computer to solve mathematical formulas and earn reward in the form of a digital currency. Their efforts help in validating the crypto-currency transactions.

The reward for verifying, bitcoin transaction, is about 25 bitcoins that translates to $22,500 when calculated using the value of the bitcoin at the time of writing this book i.e. 1 bitcoin = $912.56. This reward is awarded to the first person that solves a mathematical puzzle that helps in validating transaction.

In other words, virtual currencies have commoditized the process of validating the transactions and securing the network. The cost of the work is not paid by the people that carry out the transactions. Instead, the miners who validate the transaction are rewarded by creation of additional virtual currency.

Today, almost all online transactions make use of one or other type of virtual credit or money. The user has to pay fees for making use of the services provided by the money transfer agencies. Moreover, the online payments have to verify before the funds are transferred.

Crypto-currencies involve considerably lower costs and waiting times as when transferring the funds. The transactions are settled immediately with little waiting time. Unlike the tradition credit transaction, where the security information and credit number are transferred to the other party, the crypto-currency transaction only transfers a specific amount. There is no risk of theft of the rest of the amount unless the private key of the individual is stolen.

The virtual currency makes it possible for the individuals to buy online goods who reside in a country where there is no functioning credit system or PayPal. A large number of people in the Africa, South Asia, and Latin America don't have easy access to digital networks. By using virtual currencies such users can buy goods online without having to pay a considerable transaction fee.

Countries that don't have developed credit system become isolated from the rest of the cyber world. Crypto-currencies can serve as a big connector to the world economy.

However, the area with the biggest potential for virtual currencies lies is probably the remittances. Billions of dollars are transferred by expatriates to their country of origin. According to the World Bank, the average fee for the remittances was about 10 percent with conversion to cash often costing an additional 5 percent. The remittances are handled by different intermediaries such as wire services, banks, and currency exchanges – all of which take their cut.

By transferring the funds using the crypto-currency network, the expats will be able to save costs in transferring the money. The money can be transferred instantly through the network within a matter of minutes.

The vast majority of people in the underdeveloped regions in Africa don't have any bank account. Currently, the funds sent by the expats to these regions are not sent to the recipient's bank, but the phones using eCash. So, there will be less learning curve for the adoption of crypto-currency transfer.

While the benefits of the crypto-currency as an alternative currency are many, its proponents have yet to reassure the mass public about the legitimacy of the currency as a medium of exchange.

With the increased popularity of e-commerce and electronic transfer of payments, the demand for a virtual currency is certainly there. What is needed is to make the adoption process easier both for the merchants and for the users.

The infrastructure of virtual currencies such as bitcoin, litecoin, and others is present. However, there is a need for improvements particularly pertaining to security and legitimacy of the transactions.

If the digital currencies can make the transfer of payment more secure, it would remove the obstacle that prevents the currency from becoming a mainstream alternate mode of exchange. And once the crypto-currencies are able to achieve this goal, it would have a great effect on the world economy that will be respected as a global currency of exchange. Moreover, it will also pressure the banks and other financial institutions to bring down the cost in order to stay competitive that would greatly benefit the end-users.

The success of the crypto-currencies as an alternate currency depends on how much confidence their users have on the currencies. The more the individuals and the companies make use of the virtual currencies to carry out the transactions the more successful will they become, and even someday completely replace the traditional currencies.

The Process of Obtaining Crypto-Currencies Explained

Individuals can purchase crypto-currencies in five ways: exchange networks, locally, mining, and selling of goods and services.

Exchange Systems

Purchasing cryptocurrency through the exchange is the most convenient way to buy the currency at a fair price. The industry contains a large number of crypto-currency exchanges that offer the platform to buy and sell bitcoins.

The easiest way to fund the account is by linking a bank account to the exchange system. Moreover, a number of credit and debit card companies offer the users the option to link to a bitcoin address.

Another way to fund the account is by sending the funds directly to the exchange provider.

Most of the exchanges require that users verify the account. The account can be verified by entering the personal identification number as well as sending scanned copies of utility bills and ID cards.

Opening the crypto-currency account is much more convenient as compared to opening a bank account. You don't have to fill long forms and wait for the account opening letter and checkbooks to start using the account.

Once the identity is verified and the funds are transferred to the account, you can start trading in crypto-currency.

Anyone can buy the bitcoin by just linking the bank or credit card account or sending the funds to the exchange network.

The option is best if you want to make the online purchases without having to go through the risks of exposing the credit cards. However, the risk of using the exchange services is that the copies of the utility bills or the ID card can be used to perform identity thefts. That's why it's important that you use credible exchange systems to buy and sell the bitcoins.

Make sure to read online reviews of the bitcoin provider so that you don't inadvertently fall into a scam. Also, find out whether the system site is secure by hovering the mouse to the address bar in the top case of Google Chrome or Mozilla Firefox or the status bar at the bottom in case of Internet explorer. A secure site will have a lock icon while an unsecure site will not contain any lock icon.

Local Purchase

Buying locally may not be the quickest way to buy the virtual coins, but it ensures complete anonymity of the purchase. You can meet up with people in the bitcoin forums or local classified ads. The method of obtaining the crypto-currency is true to the spirit of peer-to-peer nature of the currency.

You won't have to verify the identity and offer personal information to purchase the currencies. This eliminates the risk of identity theft present when opening up an account with the exchanges. Some cities have local hangouts and fairs where users can get to know each other and exchange the currency. Moreover, some cities have live Bitcoin trading floor where you can haggle for the price of the bitcoin.

However, one disadvantage of buying the cryptocurrency in this manner is that some dealers charge a premium as high as 10 percent above the market price.

Also, when buying the currency locally, you should avoid handing over the cash until you receive three confirmations on the public blockchain. So, this method is not convenient as compared to buying from the exchange.

Another way you can purchase and the crypto-currency is through the purchase of wallets. The wallets can be offered by the exchanges or a sole wallet provider.

Mining

An integral part of the crypto-currency is mining. The mining process works like this:

- First, a person buys a product, say a TV, with a virtual currency.

- Next, miners using software that perform complex mathematical calculations try to verify the currency used for the transaction. It's not just one transaction that the miners verify but a number of transactions that are grouped together as 'block chain'.

- Once the miners are able to find the 'needle in a haystack' key that verifies the transaction.

The miners receive the payment as a reward for their effort and time incurred in verifying the virtual transactions.

Once a transaction has been verified, the miner has to sign the block with the private key that is used during the verification process. The miners compete with each other to solve the cryptographic puzzle first.

After the solution is found, the miner broadcasts the solution and receives a virtual currency for the effort. The reward acts as an incentive for the miners to put their efforts in discovering the solution to the cryptographic puzzle.

Selling of Goods and Services

Selling of goods and services is the obvious manner of obtaining crypto-currencies. In this case, you won't have to sign up with an exchange. You can easily obtain the bitcoins by selling the goods and services.

Digital Wallets - The Mechanism of Storing the Currency Explained

Wallets store private keys of the users. The private key identifies the users as an owner of the bitcoin. This wallet is provided by either the crypto-currency exchange or a separate entity that only offers the digital wallets.

There is different type of wallets that differ in functionality and security.

Mobile Wallets

The mobile wallets are smartphone applications that you can download. They offer a convenient way to store crypto-currency and buy and sell the goods. However, smartphone wallets are considered less secure as they can be easily hacked online. So, it's best to avoid storing large number of cryptocurrency in the mobile wallet.

Bitcoin-QT Wallet

The Bitcoin-QT Wallet is the original bitcoin client that stores the private key in the users' wallet. The wallet downloads the blockchain and can take a few days to sync. Apart from that, the key serves as a full node on the network and communicates with the miners.

Every private key is stored on the local drive by the bitcoin-QT miners. The wallet is secure as long as you have a computer with strong firewall and anti-virus protection.

For additional security, you can have the key backed up in an external drive. You should create a backup every time that you create a new public or private key with the Bitcoin QT wallet.

Hot Wallets

Hot Wallets store the private key by a third-party. The largest hot wallet provider is the Coinbase. The service makes using bitcoins easy as the user does not have to manage the private key. Also, there is no need to understand the technical nature of the cryptocurrency operations. The hot wallet provider does the task for you.

Keeping your currency in the exchange is in effect making use of a hot wallet. The private keys are kept by the exchanges in remote servers that generally incorporate high security settings.

The prime disadvantage using hot wallets is that they are a hot target for hackers. Pooling of different crypto-currencies under one address gives greater incentives for cybercriminals to attempt a heist. The Mt. Gox fiasco that we will describe a little shows the high risk of keeping crypto-currencies with a third-party provider.

Cold Wallets

Cold wallets are the most secure option of storing the crypto-currencies. The wallets look similar to a usb key but contain small screen. Cold wallets such as Trezor isolate the private keys but still allow you to send the funds over the drives.

The devices can be password protected that offers additional security. What's more, if you somehow lose the device there is a 12-word seed that can help you recover the money stored on the blockchain.

Paper Wallets

Paper wallets is another secure wallet. The wallet is hack proof which means that they cannot be stolen by the cybercriminals. You can store both public and private keys in the wallet.

While the paper wallets offer security, they do so at the expense of convenience. You have to create a new paper wallet every town you want to store additional coins. Also, if the private keys are somehow exposed to the internet, you will have to create a new paper wallet due to the security mechanism. However, a number of people think that the security of using the wallet more than makes up for the inconvenience.

Brain Wallets

The best thing about crypto-currency is that you can generate a wallet from just about anything. You can take any letters, numbers, and words to create a new wallet, and then memorize them.

In this way, you will be able to store millions of dollars in your mind. A website that allows you to generate a brain wallet is https://brainwallet.io/.

The website is a deterministic java address generator. The address generation takes place in the browser with no information sent to the website server.

You must enter a phrase or select a random phrase by clicking a button. Next you must choose whether you want to use the login info, personal info, or a generic word (geek name: salt) to create the password. The brain wallet provider uses a scrypt key derivation function to generate the address.

A disadvantage of the brain wallet is that if you forgot the address, you will lose all your money. Also, the wallet can be cracked by brute force cracking. The hackers can use a combination of words and keys in the hope of accessing the money. Once they find the right combination, you can lose your money forever.

The brain wallets need to be random in order to be safe. Also, you should consider making your own phrases instead of clicking on the random button. Consider using a phrase that is more than 8 words long. Also, keep in mind that the paraphrase and salts are case sensitive.

Lightweight Wallets

The lightweight wallets are software application that you download on your desktop computer. They are similar to mobile wallets except that the application used as a crypto-currency is desktop computer.

The benefit of lightweight wallets is that they do not require that you download the entire blockchain. A blockchain gets bigger overtime once you carry on additional transactions. The lightweight wallets allow you to store the private key more conveniently as compared to the bitcoin-QT wallet.

Moreover, the lightweight wallets contain features that are not available in the default bitcoin wallet. You do not have to create a backup every time a new address is generated. The wallet generally has a single seed that identify bitcoin address. This gives greater ease in using and storing the bitcoin addresses.

1.3 Crypto-currencies in the Market

The increased usage of crypto-currencies as an alternate mode of payment, and the ease of setting up a digital currency, has led to a large number of companies introducing their own virtual currencies.

More than 740 virtual currencies are circulating in the market. Of these, about 26 have a market capitalization of above $10 million as of 2016. [8] Here we will take a close look at the five most popular cryptocurrencies that are currently circulating in the market.

1.3.1 Bitcoin

Bitcoin was the first crypto-currency that was developed by a person named Satoshi Nakamoto. The currency was designed as an alternate and more convenient mode of payment for buying online goods.

The inventor of the currency who has still to make a public appearance had sent the digital currency in October 2008 to cryptography mailing list and was relapsed as open source software in 2009.

The Bitcoin system is at its core a peer-to-peer system where the transaction takes place directly between the users without any intermediary.

The transactions are recorded in a shared public ledger known as the blockchain and are verified by individuals using their personal computers who are connected to a network node.

Since there is no authority that oversees the transaction, the currency can be categorized as a virtual currency. At the moment, bitcoin is the largest digital crypto-currency in terms of total market value.

Individuals can obtain the digital currencies in three ways:

1. Buy the virtual currency using the national currency,

2. Accept them as a payment for product or services,

3. Mine them like gold.

The first two mode of obtaining bitcoin is self-explanatory. However, mining the bitcoin is something that is quite novel and confusing at the same time.

'Mining' is a lingo that simply means the discovery of new bitcoins. The miners are rewarded with 25 newly created coins. As of July 9, 2016, the reward for mining the bitcoin has been cut to half to 12.5 and will continue to be halved every four years.[9]

According to the site Blockchain.info, which is the top site that shows the latest bitcoin transactions in real-time, it takes about 1,789,546,951.05 attempts to find a key that verifies the bitcoin.

Despite such a large number of attempts required to mine the bitcoin, the quest for the virtual gold does not deter people from making the attempt. The 25-bitcoin reward is created every 10-minutes that show the popularity of the mining the virtual currency.

The individuals known as cryptocurrency miners contribute in keeping the systems running. They can set up their computers to take part in validating the transactions and earn a reward for their services.

People generally use software that follows a mathematical formula to validate the transactions. The mathematical formula is easily accessible and the software that uses the formula to mine currencies is open source. So, anyone can participate in the network.

1.3.2 Ethereum

Ethereum is another open source cryptocurrency that as developed by a cryptocurrency researcher named Vitalik Buerin in 2013. The blockchain based shared platform features smart contract functionality.

The digital crypto-currency is marketed by a non-profit organization named Ethereum Foundation and a Swiss company called ethereum Switzerland GmbH (EthSuisse).

Ethreum differs from bitcoin in several ways.

Firstly, the economic model is different from the bitcoin in that the 'miners' are paid a fixed amount (5 ether) ad infinitum.[10]

Also, the block time in ethereum is 12 seconds while it is 10 minutes in case of the bitcoin currency. The fast processing that is made possible due to the Ghost protocol and the use of Turing code results in faster transaction times.

The costs of transactions are also calculated differently in the case of ethereum. Transaction costs depend on the storage needs, computational complexity, and the bandwidth use. The cost of the transaction using bitcoin currency is the same for each block.

Lastly, ethereum uses the ethash hashtag algorithm to reward the miners instead of the more centralized ASICs system used in Bitcoin.

The live blockchain of ethereum was introduced on 30th July 2015.The initial release of the blockchain network supported the proof-of-work algorithm similar to bitcoin. However, it was later replaced to the proof-of-stake algorithm.

One of the highlights of the ethereum currency is the smart contacts. The smart contracts are apps that are stored in the blockchain and which are used to verify, facilitate, and enforce the transactions. The contracts are implemented using the Turing scripting language.

An issue that relates to the smart contracts that are stored on the public network is that bugs and security holes are present that cannot be reversed quickly. An example is the hacking attack of 17th June 2016 on ethereum that exploited a security flaw. While the hack attempt was blocked, it took a lot of time and showed the vulnerability of the system to malicious attacks.

The advantage of ethereum over bitcoin is that it not just a software platform. Instead, the currency system is a programming language that allows developers to create distributed applications and incorporate robust security features.

The smart contracts can be written using different languages including a derivative of Python known as Serpent. The contracts are executed by a decentralized virtual machine known as the ethereum virtual machine (EVM).

The smart contracts are stored publicly on different nodes of the blockchain. While calculating all the smart contracts at every node results in slight performance issues, it increases the overall security and stability. Moreover, the processing time of 12 seconds per block is faster as compared to bitcoin.

1.3.3 Ripple

Ripple is a digital currency developed by a company of the same name. Apart from serving as a currency exchange, the crypto-currency works as a real time gross settlement system (RTGS) and a remittance network.

The currency was created by Chris Larsen & Jed McCaleb in 2012. It is also called the Ripple Transaction Protocol (RTXP) or simply the Ripple protocol. The underlying architecture of the digital currency includes the consensus ledger, distributed open source internet protocol, and the native currency XRP (ripples).

Ripple is claimed to be a secure system that allows instant and free transfer of payments without any charge-backs. While the idea is similar to bitcoin and ethereal, the system is completely different as compared to the other digital currencies.

The transactions are verified through a consensus among the network members instead of mining. The infrastructure of Ripple was designed to minimize the use of resources to improve the execution time of the transactions.

Ripple relies on a common ledger that is managed by independent validating servers. The servers that could belong to anyone constantly compare and validate the transaction records.

A year after the launch, Ripple had announced the connection of Ripple and bitcoin protocols using the bitcoin bridge, which allow users to send Ripple payments to any bitcoin address.

The digital currency supports additional 'tokens' including frequent flier miles, commodities, fiat currency, or another unit of value such as mobile minutes.

As of 2016, it was the third largest crypto-currency in terms of market capitalization value after bitcoin and Ethereum.[11] While the Ripples' market cap of $500 million pales in comparison to $4.8 billion cap of bitcoin, the currency has grown in popularity in a very short period.

What's more, large companies such as UniCredit, Santander, and UBS have adopted the Ripple protocol as the transaction settlement infrastructure technology due to its increased security and reduced price advantages over other crypto-currencies including bitcoin.

The Ripple exchange had announced the creation of the first interbank group for international payments in September 2016. The crypto-currency initiative is supported by such large banks as Standard Chartered, Bank of America Merill Lynch, Westpac Banking Corporation, Santander, and the Royal Bank of Canada. These institutions have formed the Global Payments Steering Group (GPSG) that will oversee the creation and maintenance of rules relating to Ripple payments. The group will also formalize standards and perform other actions to improve the functionality and security of the crypto-currency.

1.3.4 Litecoin

Litecoin is a crypto-currency that was introduced by former Google engineer Charles Lee in 2011. It is a peer-to-peer open source project that has been introduced under the MIT/X11 license.

The technology behind litecoin is similar to bitcoin. The crypto-currency is not managed by a central authority. After bitcoin, bitcoin, ethereum, and ripple, litecoin is the fourth largest crypto-currency in terms of market capitalization. As of December 2016, the market capitalization of the crypto-currency stood at $177.4 million with a price of $3.6.

The main difference between bitcoin and litecoin is that it is able to generate a block in just 2.5 minutes as compared to 10 minutes of bitcoin. Another way that Litecoin is different from bitcoin is that the proof-of –work algorithm that is used to validate the discovery by the miners is entirely different.

Litecoin makes use of the Scrypt algorithm as opposed to the bitcoin's SHA-256 hash algorithm. The bitcoin's proof-of-work algorithm involves complex calculations that require parallel processing. This results in increased difficulty for the miners.

On the other hand, litecoin's scrypt algorithm makes use of simpler calculations. Scrypt requires large RAM instead of processing power.

However, the Scrypt algorithm makes it more difficult to create and more expensive to produce as compared to bitcoin. This is mainly due to the memory intensive hashing scheme of Scrypt.

Miners can validate transactions much faster with litecoin thanks mainly to its faster block generation. The faster blocktime results in reduced wait time for the merchants.

Miners that verify a transaction in litecoin are rewarded with 25 litecoins that at the present is valued at about $100. The crypto-currency that is awarded for each transaction will continue to halve after every 840,000 blocks (roughly about 4 years) until 84 million litecoins are mined. In this way, the issuing rates of the currency forms a geometric shape.

The peer-to-peer network of litecoin handles transactions and creation of the litecoins through scrypt. A block is created after miners find a hash value at which time a litecoin is created. The transactions are recorded in the litecoin blockchain.

A new block is appended to the blockchain every time a hash value is found according to the proof-of-work scheme. A large transaction generally consists of six blocks, while a small transaction requires less than six blocks.

A number of online exchanges all over the world now deal with litecoin. Most of the trading exchanges allow exchange of litecoins for euros (Yacuna, Krakem), dollars (Bitfines, 247exchange, BTC-e, BitBay, and OKCoin), and yuan (BTC China, Huobi, and OKCoin). Moreover, there are some exchanges that allow trading between bitcoins and litecoins.

1.3.5 Finance Coin

A one of its kind business-to-business version of digital currency that facilitates funds transfers, loans and payments from one party to another bypassing a financial institution, thereby extracting cost savings, and added efficiency. FinanceCoin uses a business-to-business network similar to that of peer-to-peer networks the likes of bitcoin.

The unique, highly secured business-to-business network timestamps the transactions by hashing them into a continuing chain of proof-of-work, creating a log that cannot be altered without recreating the proof-of-work.

FinanceCoin is a collection of concepts and technologies that form the basis of a digital currency ecosystem. Units of currency are called FinanceCoin, used to store and transmit value among participants in the FinanceCoin network. FinanceCoin, unlike other cryptocurrencies, is the only business-to-business electronic currency. FinanceCoin users communicate with each other using the FinanceCoin protocol via the Internet, although other connection networks can also be used. The FinanceCoin protocol stack, is a closed source program, it can be run on a wide range of computing devices, making the technology easily accessible by users.

Users can transfer FinanceCoin over the network to do just about anything that can be done with traditional fiat currencies, including buying and selling of goods, sending money to individuals or organizations, or extend credit to individuals and organizations.

FinanceCoin can be purchased, sold, collateralized and exchanged for other currencies at specialized electronic currency exchanges. FinanceCoin in a sense is the perfect form of money for the Internet because it is fast, secured and borderless.

Unlike traditional fiat currencies, FinanceCoin are entirely virtual. There are no physical coins or even digital coins per se. The coins are implied in transactions that transfer value from sender to receiver. Users of FinanceCoin own unique keys that allow them to prove ownership of transactions in the FinanceCoin network, unlocking the value to access it and transfer it to a new receiver. Those unique keys are stored in a digital wallet on each user's computer. Possession of the unique key that unlocks a transaction is the only prerequisite to spending FinanceCoin, putting the control entirely in the hands of each user, making it safe and secured.

FinanceCoin is a distributed, business to business system. As such there is no central server or point of control. FinanceCoin are created through a process called "mining," which involves competing to find solutions to mathematical problems while processing FinanceCoin transactions. Any participant in the FinanceCoin network may operate as a miner, using their computer's processing power to verify and record transactions. Essentially, FinanceCoin mining decentralizes the currency issuance and clearing functions of central banks and replaces the need for any central bank.

The FinanceCoin protocol includes built-in algorithms that regulate the mining function across the network. The difficulty of the processing task that miners must perform is to successfully record a block of transactions for the FinanceCoin network. The protocol halves the rate at which new FinanceCoins are created every five years, and limits the total number of FinanceCoins that can be created. Due to FinanceCoin's diminishing rate of issuance, over the long term, the FinanceCoin currency is deflationary. Furthermore, FinanceCoin cannot be inflated by "printing" new money above and beyond the expected issuance rate thus eliminating the risks of fiscal and monetary policies by central banks.

FinanceCoin is such a system, completely decentralized by design and free of any central authority, or point of control that can be attacked or corrupted. FinanceCoin represents the culmination of decades of research in cryptography and distributed systems. FinanceCoin was created in 2013 by Digital Bank Ltd. Digital Bank Ltd combined several prior inventions to create a completely decentralized closed-source electronic currency system. FinanceCoin was launched by Digital Bank, with the primary objective to facilitate the flow of capital and funds between Venture Capital Firms and Technology Startups or Emerging Growth Companies. First of its kind and currently the only business-to-business electronic currency, FinanceCoin has a bright future as the world embraces a digital age. FinanceCoin does not rely on a central authority for currency issuance or settlement and validation of transactions.

The key innovation was to use a distributed computation system (called a "proof-of-work" algorithm), allowing the decentralized network to arrive at consensus about the state of transactions. This solves the issue of duplicate transactions where a single currency unit can be utilized twice at the same given time. Previously, the duplicate transaction problem was a weakness of digital currency and it was addressed by clearing all transactions through a central clearing house.

The FinanceCoin network started in 2013, based on a reference implementation by Digital Bank Ltd. The distributed computation that provides security and resilience for FinanceCoin has increased exponentially, and now exceeds that combined processing capacity of many of the world's top super-computers. FinanceCoin's total market value is estimated between 120 to 140 million US dollars, depending on the FinanceCoin-to-dollar exchange rate. The largest transaction processed so far by the network was 45 million US dollars, transmitted instantly and processed without any fees.

The future of FinanceCoin will be an interesting and exciting one to look forward to. FinanceCoin developers have major plans in the works for FinanceCoin – to be used as digital currency in corporate mergers & acquisition (M&A) activities, real estate investment trusts (REITs), mutual funds, fixed income, equities, and commodities trading, as holding currency on online payment gateway platform, automobile trading, medical expenses, taxation matters and payment of insurance premiums, online shopping and gaming. FinanceCoin the name of the protocol, a network, and a distributed computing innovation.

The FinanceCoin currency is merely the first application of this invention. As a developer, I see FinanceCoin as akin to the Internet of money, a network for propagating value and securing the ownership of digital assets via distributed computation. There is a lot more to FinanceCoin than meets the eye and I will be eagerly waiting and anticipating to watch this one of its kind business-to-business electronic currency.

1.4   General Features of Crypto-currencies

Crypto-currencies have certain basic features that differentiate them from fiat currencies. An understanding of the inherent properties is important to fully grasp the disruption caused by the digital currencies.

1. Decentralized Exchange Medium

Bitcoins and other similar digital currencies are printed electronically. Unlike the paper currency, digital currencies are not controlled by the central bank of any country. The individuals mine bitcoins and work together to make the system work.

This means that the central banks can't tinker with a value of money using the monetary policy or simply take them away from people similar to what the Central European Bank in Cyprus did in 2013.[12] The money in the bitcoin exchange, on the other hand, keeps on flowing even if a network goes down.

They exchange does not depend on the central bank for the issuance or supply of the currency. No one has any control over the creation of the virtual currency. The digital currencies are created by individuals for carrying out transactions.

2. A Cap on Digital Currency

The virtual currencies have a market cap on them. The Bitcoin technical system created by Satoshi Nakamoto on which all other digital currencies are based can never have more than 21 million coins in circulation. This is unlike the traditional fiat currencies that have no cap as to how much they can be printed by the central government.

As a result, the value of digital currencies cannot be artificially manipulated by the government. The value is determined by the demand and supply as opposed to the amount of currency in circulation.

3. No Third-Party

A highlight of the digital currency is that a third-party is not required in transferring of the payments. There is no need of MasterCard, PayPal, or check to transfer the funds.

As a result, you don't have to pay any fees or divulge your real identity when transferring the money to another individual.

4. Limited Supply

The supply of crypto-currencies is limited that is not in the control of the central bank, private banks, or other financial regulatory authority. Since there is no governmental control over the supply, the currencies cannot be used for the monetary policy goals of inflation or deflation.

All of the crypto-currencies' supply is limited according to the coded schedule. The supply of the crypto-currency can be determined at any given time in the future.

5. Anonymous Transactions

The transactions made using virtual currencies are completely anonymous. While the transactions are publicly displayed, no one can trace the owners. As a result, you won't have to worry about an organization tracing the source of the funds.

The anonymity feature of the crypto-currencies is at once a risk and attraction for the public. With increased usage of the crypto-currency will come greater scrutiny by the financial and legal authorities. Exchanges may be required to comply with the requirements of know-your-customer (KYC) controls and anti-money laundering (AML) statutes.

Also, the identity of the users that access the currency through an exchange or wallet service have to be verified. This makes them no different from opening a bank account. However, the loss of identity takes place at the point of entry and not at the point of execution of the transaction.

People that wish to take advantage of the intrinsic anonymity of the crypto-currency have to look for other methods of obtaining the coins such as taking part in mining, obtaining the bitcoin in a private transaction, or as a compensation of providing the goods or services. In these situations, anonymity can be maintained when carrying out a transaction as the crypto-currency verification process does not record the identity of the user on a ledger. The only user-related information contained in the blockchain is the currency address. The corresponding keys are held by the owners as a proof of the ownership.

Maintaining anonymity, however, is not guaranteed even in case alternate methods are used to obtain the digital currency that doesn't require identity verification. Even if a person acquires digital currency without divulging personal information, the real world identity can still be traced within the network.

Academic researchers that had created the systems are now working with law enforcement agencies to help nab criminals. The experts operate in a new field that represents a combination of forensics, economics, and computer science.

These experts had helped in uncovering and busting the site Silk Road that was found to be involved in money laundering and illegal drug trade.

The bitcoin blockchain ledger consists of record of transactions that are nothing more than numbers and letters. For instance, the "1Ez69SnzzmePmZX3WpEzMKTrcBF2gpNQ55" represented nearly $20 million (or 30,000 bitcoin) that were seized during the Silk Road bust.

The real-world identity can be revealed by inspecting the IP addresses of the computers that were used in making the transactions. Once the IP address of the computer where the transaction originates is known, the real-world identity can be exposed as well.

6. Irrevocable Payments

The payments that are made using crypto-currencies are irrevocable. The buyers once they have made a payment cannot take back the amount from the seller. This is at once the benefit and a risk of the digital currency.

While it offers comfort to the sellers in that once they receive the payment, it will remain in their coffers. The buyer can't take back the paid amount under the authorization of a court order or by any other means.

7. Global Currency

Virtual currency is not owned by a central bank of any country. It is truly a global currency that is owned by the individuals. The currency can be used to purchase just about anything that is sold online from anywhere in the world. The payments are processed almost instantly within a matter of minutes.

Crypto-currencies represent the next step in payments for goods and services. They are the most powerful innovation today in terms of disruption and utility. Now that you know about the basic features of the crypto-currencies, let's find out the benefits and risks of the digital currencies.

1.5 The Benefits and the Risks

Crypto-currencies are a currency similar to the fiat currency. The virtual currency solves many of the problems that are associated with the paper-based currencies. The benefits that set the digital currencies apart from the government-backed currencies include the following.

1. Easy to Establish

The financial institutions require their customers to fulfill a number of requirements such as filling the forms, submitting the documents, and verification of identity before setting up an account.

In contrast, setting up digital currency address is much easier. You can establish a virtual address within seconds without divulging your identity or depositing any amount.

2. Transparent Transactions

All the transactions made using the digital currency are transparent. The network keeps a record of every single – big or small transaction – that is carried in the network.

The information is contained in a huge virtual ledger that is known as the blockchain. The blockchain reveals all.

Anyone can tell how many virtual currencies are stored at a particular address and what they have been used to purchase. However, the exchange network does not show who owns the address.

People that won't want to get unneeded attention in the virtual world can use a different address such as not using the same address for making the purchase or storing a large number of virtual currencies at any one address.

2. Fees are Minimal

Banks charge fees for international transfer of payments. The same is not the case in the virtual exchange networks. Individuals can transfer funds from one country to another without having to pay any fees at all. This is the main reason that the virtual currencies are getting popular particularly among the businessmen in that they incur great savings in costs involved in the transfer of a large amount of money.

The process of sending, receiving, and verification of virtual currency are all conducted by the individuals instead of a third-party institution. Users contribute to the network by sharing the burden of authorizing the transactions. The shared nature of the digital currency exchange system results in minuscule transaction costs.

3. Fast Process

Another great benefit of digital currencies is that the transaction happens in quick time. You can easily transfer money within minutes. In contrast transferring money using the traditional means such as PayPal, credit cards can take days. The process is slow and a rather complicated.

With digital currencies, once you obtain the currencies you can make the payment and have it verified within minutes. The fast payment processing creates convenience for both parties of the transaction.

4. No Risk of Seizure

Traditional currencies can be seized by the government for a reason. The same is not true for digital currencies. Government officials can't order a freeze of the wealth. The individuals have total freedom about what they do with the virtual money.

5. Perfect Anonymity

Another benefit of the digital currencies over traditional currencies is that users can maintain perfect anonymity. Unless users publicly announce their address, no one can know about the owner. Also, in case the name of the owner is publicized, a new address can be created to maintain anonymity.

In contrast, third-parties can gain access to personal financial data in case of the traditional method of payments. The information can be used for advertising or even malicious causes. Also, changing the personal address or the institution that holds the funds are time-consuming and costly tasks for an individual.

6. Safe and Secure

Virtual currency exchange systems are generally more secure as compared to traditional payment systems. Unlike the traditional credit and debit instruments that require only a few verifications to gain access to the funds, gaining access to the virtual currency is hard.

The virtual currency can be stolen only if the user's computer is hacked and the private key is obtained. As long as a person has the sole ownership of the private key, no one can steal money from the account.

The public blockchain ledger is not stored in a single location. It is distributed across different computers. So, in theory, the data is invulnerable to attack similar to a bank data that is located on a central server. It is a gargantuan task for anyone to hack thousands of commuters at the same time. Also, there is no risk of an insider manipulating the software of the central server. This makes the virtual currencies a reliable means of exchange.

7. Low Inflation Risk

Due to the limited supply, the crypto-currencies solve one of the most pressing problems of our time: the loss of the monetary value or purchasing power of the currency over time due to the additional printing of money by the government.

Since the virtual currencies have a cap, they can't grow indefinitely. The creation of new currency will decrease and will stop within a few decades. As a result, the risk of hyper-inflation is low with the digital currencies.

8. Low Risk of Collapse

Fiat currencies depend on the governments that occasionally go bankrupt. In addition, the events such hyperinflation results in the collapse of the monetary system as it can wipe out the value of lifetime savings of the individuals.

With crypto-currencies, the risk of collapse while present is much lower. The currency is not created or regulated by any government. Its global nature makes it resilient to monetary collapse.

9. No Taxation

Due to the technical nature of the exchange and less oversight by the central banks, there is no way to implement taxation on the virtual currency.

While digital currencies act as a currency in both theoretical and practical respect, the basic tax rules that were prescribed by the IRS in 2014 treats the currency as a property. So, if a person buys the virtual currency for $200, and later the value has increased to $500, the gain of $300 has to be reported for tax purposes.

The catch is that it's not possible at present for the IRS to trace the users of the transactions. So, digital currency transactions are not taxable at the moment. And this same applies in other countries as well.

That being said, a person with a strong civic sense can voluntarily send a payment to the tax authorities.

10. Universal Medium of Exchange

Digital currency is an international currency that eliminates the exchange rate problem. The different rates of the currencies create 'artificial' increase and decrease in the prices of goods that are imported from abroad.

A decrease in the exchange rate of a currency with respect to another currency makes the goods expensive for the buyers that use the devalued currency to purchase the goods.

The 'artificial' increase and decrease in prices is contrary to the interest of not just the buyers, but also the sellers.

Digital currencies are not haunted by fluctuating exchange rate. They represent a true form of international currency that people can use anywhere in the world.

11. Open Source Code

The code of virtual currencies such as bitcoin is open source. As a result, the modules can be easily created and implemented for different devices. Also, it provides users with different experiences to contribute to the development of the system. The open source nature of the digital currencies facilitates a greater number of people to collaborate, test, and participate in the digital currency revolution.

From the above discussion, you should've realized that there is a lot going for the digital currencies.

The decentralized nature of the exchange, minimum costs, no requirement of a third-party, transparent transactions, and a unified international currency are some of the prime factors that have resulted in growing popularity of the virtual currency as an alternate mode of payment.

While the benefits are many, the crypto-currencies are associated with certain risks as well.

1. Fluctuating Market Value

While the value of the digital currencies is not affected by the exchange rate changes, they are not immune to change in value. In fact, digital currencies experience great fluctuations due to the demand. The value of the currency declines in case fewer users are using them to carry on the transactions.

The factors that have affected the digital currency values in the past include:

- Huge losses due to malware attacks on account of poor security measures

- Government rules restricting the use of digital currency

- Hacking of the digital currency systems

- A shutdown of a large digital market such as Silkroute

Apart from the above main factors, there is evidence that media coverage of the controversial aspect of the virtual currencies such exchange collapses, criminal activity, and others also result in a fluctuating market value.

2. Risk from Cybercriminals

Another issue with digital currencies is that they are not entirely safe from cyber criminals. Once the hackers obtain the private encryption key by hacking into the system, they can use the key to transferring the amount to their accounts. And what's worse is that this transfer is irreversible, which means it's next to impossible to get back the stolen amount.

3. Growing Government Regulations

At the moment, the virtual currency is not regulated by the central banks. But the link with criminal transactions is forcing some governments to create regulations regarding the digital currency. Once the government regulates the virtual currency at the national level it won't be any different than the paper currency.

4. High Risk of Loss

Some people invest in digital currencies similar to investing in foreign exchanges with the aim of making a profit from the fluctuating value. However, investment in digital currencies is not covered by any federal program. This means that a collapse in the value of the digital currency could wipe out the entire investment amount. Also, you won't be able to avail taxation benefits that are applicable to security investors. So, you should think twice before investing in digital currencies to grow your wealth.

5. Criminal Activity

Due to the anonymity of the transactions, the digital currency has been the preferred method for criminals. The criminals are increasingly using the currency as it's impossible to trace the parties involved in the transaction. If the trend continues, it is possible that the government agencies will place a ban on the currencies in the respective countries.

Like any other new technology, it's not surprising that digital currency has certain risks. But this does not mean that the currency is doomed to fail.

A number of breakthrough improvements are continuously being announced in the core software program to make the system secure and stable. The copyright-free nature of the digital currency means that it is accessible to a large number of individuals who can peer inside, offer improvements, and create modules that solve different problems.

1.6   Impact of the Digital Currency Revolution

The digital currency is gaining acceptance not just among the individuals but most importantly among a large number of commercial enterprises as well.

Today a number of well-renowned companies such as Reddit, WordPress, OkCupid, and Foodler are accepting digital currencies as a payment for their services. Some of the companies had even announced that they will pay salaries to the employees using eh crypto-currency.

While the idea of the digital currency had first emerged about two decades ago with the likes of CyberCash and DigiCash, the initiative has proved successful only recently after the release of Bitcoin.

And the reason is obvious. The markets today are more receptive of the virtual currency due to the advancement of internet technologies. While the critics are foretelling the doom of the digital currency, the reality is that the technology is here to stay.

The fact is that increasing number of large companies are adopting the technology to smooth line the payment process and gain from the cost savings. And this trend is increasing year-by-year as developers continue to unveil better and improved virtual currencies.

The digital currencies represent much more than alternate currencies. They are a radically innovative and rather disruptive technology system that is changing the way value is exchanged in the society. It is not far from the truth when we say that virtual currencies are simply the most powerful financial innovation in the past 500 years.

When applied at the grass root level of the global economy, the system could cut trillions in transaction fees and automate the work that is done by government property-title offices, payment processors, accountants, and lawyers.

The most powerful way that the digital currencies are impacting the society is by offering opportunities for billions of people to transfer money in a more convenient manner.

It's true that the adoption of the digital currency has been suppressed by negative news such as the closure of a digital currency medium known as Silk Road by the FBI in 2013 as it was used by a large number of criminal gangs. Moreover, the news about millions of virtual currencies being lost in a Tokyo-based bitcoin exchange system known as Mt. Gox in 2014 had a negative impact on the adoption of the digital currency.

However, people have not ditched the digital currency altogether. In fact, some investors even see bright years ahead for the digital currency. LinkedIn founder Reid Hoffman and Netscape founder Marc Andreesen had invested about $315 million in digital currency-related projects in 2014, which was triple the amount venture-capital investment related to digital currencies in 2013.

In addition, the digital wallet provider had stated that the year 2015 had started with an injection of $75 million in the digital currency projects by investors that included the Spanish bank Banco Bilbao Vizcaya Argentaria as well as the New York Stock Exchange.

Developers are building digital-currency tools for the world's 2.5 billion "unbanked" people, in a bid to bring them into the global financial system. Others are packing additional information into the core programs to create applications well beyond currency transfers: software-managed "smart contracts" that need no lawyers, automated databases of digital assets and copyright claims, peer-to-peer property transfers and electronic voting systems that can't be rigged.

The digital currency incentive schemes and distributed ledger technologies have created a radical new model of exchanging payments between two or more parties. The main factor that has contributed to the increasing popularity of the peer-to-peer exchange system is the efficiencies in the form of reduced transaction costs and time particularly in the case of international transactions.

Beyond the transfer of funds, the digital currency technologies have impacted a wide range of financial markets as well as infrastructure resulting in secure and accurate record keeping for different parties.

The introduction of more stable and robust currency systems (both existing and in the pipeline) has made the system more stable and attractive for such diverse financial players as security exchanges, trade repositories, security depositories, and even governmental organizations.

The growing use of the distributed ledger system has attracted the attention of regulators and policymakers both at the national and international levels.

The IRS has requested through the Department of Justice to allow it to gain access to the identity of users that use the system for tax purposes. Recently it had ordered the San Francisco-based Coinbase to hand over the identity of millions of users that trade using the virtual currencies.

The digital currencies have greatly disrupted the existing business model and resulted in radical ways to make payments. However, the currency has received the much-needed boost not from the users in the US but those in the far-east including China.

Digital currencies are considered the 'People's Right' in China with the People's Bank of China having announced its intention of creating a sovereign digital currency. Bitcoin presents as an ideal alternative for fund transfer and investment by the Chinese due to strict capital control.

The only countries that have banned the use of bitcoin include Bangladesh, Bolivia, Ecuador, and the Kyrgyz Republic. The rest allow the users to use virtual currencies for trading goods and services. In fact, Japan is one of the few countries that recognize digital currencies as an alternate mode of monies.

The policymakers in the US have tried to address a balance between overregulation and the abuses and risks of the digital currencies. The Commodity Futures Trading Commission (CFTC) has classified the digital currency as a commodity. In addition, the US Treasury regards the crypto-currency as a decentralized, convertible virtual currency. Also, a magistrate judge in the state of Texas had ruled that bitcoins are currency or a form of money within the plain meaning of the term and were subject to the jurisdiction of the court.

The initial focus of the regulatory authorities is on the most pressing relating to the individuals that include:

- Investor / Consumer protection

- Tax evasion

- Financial integrity

Due to the inherent nature of the digital currencies, several different types of regulators are involved at the national level.

Since, digital currencies combine the features of properties, currencies, and payment systems; this will have implications in their regulatory and legal treatment and the national agencies that should regulate them.

The digital currencies operate in a virtual world that increases the risks of regulatory arbitrage. This has increased the need for effective policy coordination at both the national and international level.

1.7 Conditions for a Successful Cryptocurrency

Digital currencies represent the latest evolution of exchange system. The fact cannot be denied that digital currencies have created a lot of opportunities in streamlining the payment process. It has cut the time and effort required for processing and validation of payments.

That being said, a lot needs to be done for the cryptocurrency to become successful at the mass scale.

For the successful adoption of crypto-currency, the role played by all kinds of online businesses and trading platforms cannot be denied. In other words, socializing of the crypto-currency over the internet is an essential condition of its success.

In addition, there is increased need of transparency relating to the digital currency system. Rules should also be made to address the uncertainties and disruptions that result in losses for the users.

The disruptions can relate to either the technological system or the overall market. These include risk related to the digital currency exchange platforms, wallet providers, and payment processors. Since most of these systems are not regulated, it makes the customers vulnerable to exploitation and attacks.

Although, the virtual currencies have experienced wide-scale popularity, they have been a target of attacks due to the same reasons. Thefts have occurred by hacking into the virtual currency exchanges storage network including the Mt. Gox hacking that we had mentioned earlier.

In addition, hackers have used malware programs such as the remote access stealing malware (CCSM) and remote access Trojans (RAT) to break into user's computers and steal the wallets.

Some of the preventive measures that can be taken include:

- Monitoring of the digital currency systems

- Obligations to report suspicious activities

- Record keeping of every transaction

The above measure if made park of the national Anti-Money Laundering (AML) and Combating the Financing of Terrorism (CFT) frameworks. The main challenge, however, in implementing policies to deter fraud in relation to digital currency relates to assigning the responsibility: whether they should be borne by the user or the exchange mediums.

Another condition for the success of crypto-currency includes the use of increased security system. For instance, threshold cryptography technique can be used whereby the private keys are split into different parts that are stored in a different location such as on the cloud, the smartphone, and the desktop. The task of accessing the keys becomes theoretically improbable once they are located in different places.

Another technique that can be used in deterring the cyber-attack includes Super Wallets. The supper wallet should act as a bank that stores users' private keys using the threshold cryptography technique. Also, users can carry divide the funds into sub-wallet that contain the small sum of money and money should be transferred from the super wallet once required.

Other solution to prevent theft of private keys includes generating not one but random keys, incorporate password based encryption, installing industry standard firewall software, and using hardware devices such as Trusted Patch Device that protect cryptographic data from malware attack.

Apart from criminal attacks, the virtual currency system also faces the risk of accidental loss of money due to human errors or system failures. A simple solution to overcome the problem is to create a backup and keeping them safe using the cryptographic techniques.

The anonymity of users is one of the plus points of the digital currency ecosystem. A user can be identified by nothing more than a virtual address. Moreover, users can maintain different addresses that are not linked to each other.

However, a problem is that the trust concept is breached at the regulatory level due to placing increased emphasis on anonymity. The remedy is to create a balance between the anonymity and trust level for the users. The exchange mediums must create a policy to divulge only that details of the users to the regulatory authorities that are needed for taxation purposes.

A major negative point of the virtual currencies is that the payments are irreversible. This prevents any action to be taken in case the buyer has been cheated by the seller.

A turnaround for this problem is by making use of protocols that encourages fair trade between the parties. The approach consists of creating three types of transactions:

- Regular transaction

- Refund transaction

- Claim transaction

The probability that the user will cheat is less when the transaction can go through all of above stages. The refund transaction and claim stage will ensure that the user has a course of reprieve in the case of being wronged by the seller.

In the regular transaction stage, both the parties can exchange private signatures that will help in establishing trusts. In addition, the parties must agree to a claim or refund as an option before executing the transaction.

The fact that blockchain technology is a public dataset increases the possibility of exploitation. However, national and private institutions have vested interest in eliminating the risks and promoting the technology.

That is the reason that apart from a couple of countries most others have not altogether deemed the system as illegal. Crypto-currency with all their loopholes and vulnerabilities remain an innovative and attractive alternate medium of exchange.

However, once the cryptocurrency developers and regulators contribute in implementing strict control policies, the risk of the system will become negligible.

Developers need to know how to create robust systems that are thoroughly tested against hacks. They need to improve the system to the point that it becomes impenetrable. Once the flaws of the system are ironed out through improved security measures and regulations, the crypto-currency may well replace fiat and credit currencies as fast and efficient alternative medium of exchange.

The exchange systems need to implement standardized smart technologies to bulletproof against hacker attacks. This is the only way that crypto-currencies can gain mass scale acceptance as a popular, economical, and efficient medium of exchanging goods between the parties.

The risk that a virtual vault could be plundered or the laptop crash erasing millions of dollars needs to be reduced through improved modules that are built on the existing technology.

One final condition that can spell success of the crypto-currency is the absence of increased control and regulations regarding the digital currency. The main reason that crypto-currency have enjoyed increased popularity is the low government scrutiny and anonymity of the transactions. Increased control of the government will erode the original premise that led to the very existence of crypto-currency.

At this point while the number of merchants that accept the virtual currency has increased, there are still in the minority. For the virtual currency to gain increased acceptance the above-mentioned conditions must be met. Otherwise, the radical new technology can be just another fad that fades away a few years after its inception.

1.8 Future Prospects and Conclusion

The concept of digital currencies has created a disruption in the financial, economic, and technological world. Digital currencies have provided a more convenient alternative to the users to exchange the goods and services.

An increasing number of merchants and financial corporations are adopting the technology to streamline the exchange process. The success of the digital currency can be attributed to different factors. The minimal transaction fees, decentralized nature of the exchange and fast payment processing are some of the main reasons for increased popularity of the payment medium.

Having said that, there are certain flaws or pain points that once properly addressed can result in increased probability of adaptability of the payment platform as a prime medium of exchange.

The open source and independent nature of the payment platform provide an opportunity for collaborative efforts in addressing the flaws of the system. Once all the issues are resolved, it is hoped that the digital currency revolution will continue for the long run offering economical advantages and anonymity in carrying out the transactions.

What excites most about the digital currency revolution is that the future application of the technology is extremely broad. The current development in the core digital currency development can be compared with the development of Internet Protocols (IP) in the 80s that paved way for the online medium to be adopted as a prime e-commerce platform.

Already a large number of apps have been made that make use of the crypto-currency blockchain architecture. In a way, the digital currency system has become a kind of an open-source operating system that can host different powerful apps that help facilitate the exchange.

So, is crypto-currency merely a fad, or do they represent a major evolution of the exchange system?

At the moment, only time will tell whether the digital currencies such as bitcoin and others will be successful in the future. However, one thing is certain that the future does look promising for the virtual currencies.

Ever since the digital currency system came to prominence in 2009, it had commanded the attention of both the media and the financial experts.

The currency had exploited strong encryption algorithm to create a radically new exchange medium. The identity of the users is shielded using a pseudonym similar to the origin of the crypto-currency that remains a mystery as the person with the alias Satoshi Nakamoto has not been revealed to the public. But no matter how shadowy the origin the future looks promising for the digital currency.

At the present, the market cap of Bitcoin amounts to $14 billion. Other alternative digital currencies also have a large market cap with Ethereum, Ripple, and Litecoin having a cap about $937 million, $224 million, and $194, respectively. There are dozens of other digital currencies having market cap in excess of $1 million. And the great fact about the digital currencies is that no one is in charge of the currency – not banks, not the governments, not even the founders. The real control of the currency is in the hands of the users who collectively manage the currency deriving mutual benefits.

The system has also drawn attention from large financial institutions including JP Morgan Chase. They are increasingly looking at the exchange payment platform to reduce the transaction costs and streamline the internal payment systems.

The popularity of the virtual currency among the mainstream target market has resulted in the creation of above 700 crypto-currencies; all of which are based on the original concept of bitcoin put forward by Nakamoto.

What's more, in 2016, digital currency officially made its mark in the academic field with the launch of Ledger, the first journal that is dedicated to the research of crypto-currency.

The blockchain technology represents public database that offers convenience to the individual buyer and sellers. Companies have adopted the bitcoin blockchain concept and built abstracted layers on top of the system.

CHAPTER TWO

Is Crypto-Currency a Real Currency? An Economic Insight

2.1 Introduction

Digital currencies such as bitcoin and others have been described in the mainstream media in different ways: a form of investment, exchange system, and most recently crypto-currency.

But the question remains: are they a real currency?

In order to answer this question, we have to take a step back in time and read about the origin of the crypto-currency that had started digital currency revolution – Bitcoin.

2.2 History and Background of Bitcoin

The idea about bitcoin was first described by a person with the alias Satoshi Nakamoto in 2008 that was titled 'Bitcoin: A Peer-to-peer Electronic Cash System.

The paper informed the readers about the method to use a peer-to-peer network for creating a system to generate 'a system for electronic transactions without relying on trust.'

The technology on which the digital currency bitcoin is based does not represent a radical innovation. The electronic cash protocols were developed

David Chaum while the hascash and the proof-of-work codes were processed by Stefan Brands. In addition, the distributed scarcity based crypto-currencies including bit gold developed by Nick Szabo and b-money of Wei Dai had already been developed.

What the creator of bitcoin did was to unify the different existing technologies and introduced a practical version of the crypto-currency.

The introduction of the virtual currency might have been in reaction to the 2008 financial crisis as Nakamoto who is believed to be the creator of the currency had posted a note in the bitcoin network database that read: "The Times 03/Jan/2009 Chancellor on brink of second bailout for banks."

The bitcoin network along with the open source bitcoin client was created in January 2009. And the first ever bitcoin was mined by Nakamoto who earned a reward of 50 bitcoins.

Afterwards, the first transaction was conducted by a Florida bitcoin miner named Laszlo Hanyecz when he paid 10,000 BTC - $25 today - for Papa John's pizza.

By the end of 2010, the transaction using bitcoins had exceeded $1 million. Later in 2011, BitPay introduced a smartphone wallet. A year later the merchant service provider had revealed that more than 1,000 merchants were using the payment processing system of the company.

The virtual currency gained a wide exposure in 2012 and 2013 when more retailers began accepting the virtual currency.

The value of bitcoin really started to take off in 2013. The currency had started the year at $13.50 per bitcoin, but it had rocketed upwards to around $220 per bitcoin by April of that year.

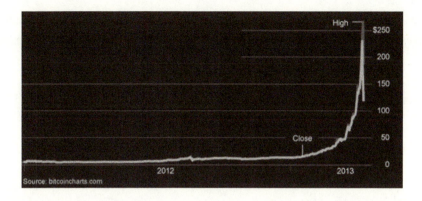

Source: bitcoincharts.com

The price of the bitcoins started to get very volatile after reaching the highs in 2013. The price had dipped to $70 by the middle of that year and then increased to over $1,216.73 by the end of November, which is an all-time high record value of the bitcoin.

At this time around Silk Road website that used bitcoins was found to be involved in black market transactions including narcotics and money laundering, and was shut down by the FBI.

In October 2013, the world's first bitcoin ATM was introduced in Vancouver, in British Columbia in Canada by Robocoin and Bitcoiniacs. A month later the University of Nicosia in Cyprus had stated that it will accept bitcoins as tuition fees.

A dramatic development in the history of the bitcoin came in 2014 when the Japanese based Mt. Gox, the worlds' largest bitcoin exchange, had announced that the hackers had apparently stolen $460 million from its account while a further $27.4 million dollar were missing from the account. The company had filed for bankruptcy in the same year.

The virtual currency had received a seal of approval as a 'convertible decentralized virtual currency' from the US Treasury in August 2013. Moreover, German Finance Minister had ruled out that bitcoin is a 'unit of account' and therefore subject to tax and legal ramifications.

The 2016 has been a year of revival for the bitcoin. The price of the bitcoin had increased from $433.59 to around $968.23 by the end of the year, an increase of nearly 55 percent.

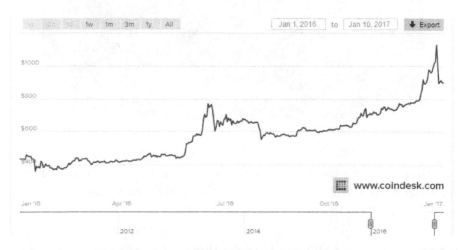

The increasing desire for a cost effective and faster alternative exchange system has led to the increased popularity of the digital currency. The public including the individuals and the merchants are increasingly accepting bitcoin as an alternate mode of payment. The Nakamoto legacy that represents a decentralized digital currency not linked to government fiat money has made a great reverberation in the financial, economic, and technological world and will continue to do so in the coming decades.

2.3 Bitcoin's Weaknesses as a Currency

Charles Mackay in his Memoirs of extraordinary popular delusions and the madness of crowds written in 1852 had stated that money is most often a cause of delusion for the masses.

The problem with fiat currency is that it is almost entirely based upon trust. The creator of bitcoin Nakamoto had argued that the main issue with the paper currency is that the central bank that we trust not to debase the currency has been guilty of breaches in the past. Banks lend out the money held in the account in waves of credit bubbles. This result is a vicious cycle of busts whereby people lose their hard-earned money at no cause of their own.

The best thing about Bitcoin is that it's the world's first truly decentralized and distributed virtual currency. The digital currency was introduced in order to solve the negative points of the fiat currency through the application of internet and communication technologies.

The digital currency is independent of the control of a centralized institution. In a way, the digital currency is a democratic currency is owned and managed by the people.

With digital currencies, including bitcoin, there is no fear of a bank declaring bankruptcy and taking with it hard earned money of a large number of individuals.

Bitcoin solves the trust issue by making the transactions publicly known to the individuals within the bitcoin network. Every transaction is recorded in a public ledger that can be accessed by just about anyone. What's more the participants work together to sustain the system.

The digital currency involves no intermediaries such as banks or other financial institutions such as PayPal, Visa, or MasterCard. The digital currency can be transferred from one place to another quickly and in a cost-effective manner.

Currency as a mode of payment is a consensual system that was developed to solve the issues of barter-based society. Previously gold and silver were the de-facto currencies that were replaced by paper currency.

Bitcoin represents the most recent advancements in the mode of payment. The digital currency fulfills the five core attributes of a currency viz portability, a store of value, a measure of value, divisibility, and a medium of exchange.

The digital currency has all the positive features of a fiat currency save for not being declared a legal tender. Apart from that there are certain limitations or weaknesses of the virtual currency that should be overcome before the currency can be regarded as a true alternative or replacement of the fiat currency.

At the present, the world of cryptocurrency is like the Wild West containing both the good and the bad guys. Due to no regulations and certain security loopholes, the system is open to abuse by the bad guys who are bent on gaining access to 'easy money' by robbing legitimate owners of the bitcoins.

Since the system is a fairly new one, a number of unknown and unexploited security flaws are present. A person with a malicious intent and technical knowledge of the bitcoin infrastructure can easily gain access to tremendous amount of wealth.

Apart from the potential of security breaches, another significant weakness of the virtual currency is that it is subject to extreme fluctuations. The constant fluctuations cause confusion particularly when a refund is being sought. For instance, if a shirt has been purchased for 2.5 BTC but afterwards the value of the bitcoin has decreased.

So, should the person seek 2.5 BTC or a new amount? Which currency should the BTC be pegged to when calculating the currency valuation? These are some of the questions about which there is still not consensus.

Then there is the problem in that virtual currency is only accepted by a minority of online merchants. As a result, bitcoins cannot be regarded as a replacement of the fiat currency.

Another weakness of bitcoins is that at the moment they always have to be pegged to particular currency when making transactions. On its own, the virtual currency cannot be relied upon since it does not have a stable value.

In addition, the virtual currency has no physical form. A person can lose the data is infected by a virus or the hard drive crashes. In such a situation, all the bitcoins of the person will be lost forever. There is no way of recovery of the amount that can easily bankrupt the investor.

What's more there is no buyer protection when the digital currency is used to make the payments. Once a payment is made, the transaction cannot be reversed. There is a possibility of using a third-party escrow services such as Clear Coin. But this would trump the benefits of the digital currency as the escorw services will act similar to a bank resulting in increased transaction costs.

Another weakness of the digital currency is that there is no guarantee of the minimum valuation by any centralized authority. If a large number of bitcoin investors decide to leave the system, the value of the currency will fall significantly. So, the decentralized nature of the digital currency is both a blessing and a weakness at the same time.

Deflation is a pressing concern for central banks. It stalls the economic activity in a country leading to low economic activity and high unemployment. Since the total supply of bitcoins is fixed at 21 million, it prevents the prospect of high inflation but also raises the possibility of a deflation. The supply cap will make people reluctant to spend money.

In the end, bitcoin provides tremendous benefits as a medium of exchange. However, a lot of work is required at both the local and the national level for the success of the currency. There is a requirement of implementation of improved cryptographic techniques to overcome the weaknesses of the currency.

The combination of crypto techniques and improved regulations relating to the currency to address the issues of abuse could pave way for a radical new form of currency that offers a fast, economical, and more convenient option for the exchange of goods and transfer of funds.

2.4 Conclusion: Obstacles Faced by Bitcoin

Bitcoin have been in existence for several years. However, a lot is required for its mainstream acceptance. Unless the issues relating to the digital currencies are not resolved, the currency will continue to be adopted by only a minority segment of the society.

The good thing is that there is increased interest particularly at the corporate level of developing not just the currency but also the technology that is based on the blockchain.

With great advancements made in the development of the digital currency, it's seems unlikely that the currency will collapse overnight.

The fundamental question is how the obstacles and challenges are overcome that paves way for worldwide acceptance of the electronic currency.

The main obstacle that prevents mainstream acceptance of the digital currency relates to the potential for abuse due to security loopholes as well as lack of regulations regarding the digital currencies.

The anonymous nature of the currency has attracted the wrong type people who look to gain money through pump-and-dump schemes, illegal activities, and shady crypto-exchanges. The digital currency has also become the preferred mode of exchange for money laundering and other criminal activities such as drug deals and even an assassination market.

The negative publicity of the digital currency has earned the ire of government officials with some countries even banning the use of the currency.

Another obstacle faced by bitcoin is the extreme fluctuation in the prices. The volatility of the currency is in fact the prime reason that it has not been used by majority of the people. A currency needs to be relatively stable for it to be usable. The high volatility of the digital currency at the moment makes it act similar to an investment instrument instead of a currency.

Also, while a number of merchants now accept bitcoins as payments, most large players such as Apple, Google, and Wall-Mart do not accept bitcoins. This prevents the virtual currency from being accepted by the mainstream target market.

Whether the community eventually adopts bitcoins as the de facto currency is not known for certain. But things certainly look promising.

Bitcoin and alternative crypto-currencies have gained billion-dollar market cap within just a few years. While the obstacles are present that limit the potential of the digital currency, but they can be overcome through a concentrated effort at both the national and corporate level.

Around just three decades ago, the idea that people would buy goods from the comfort of their own homes seemed ludicrous. Today, however, most of the people particularly in the developed western world prefer buying goods online.

The idea of crypto-currencies is novel and radical at the same time. That's the reason that it is not immune to unfavorable and negative public perception. People have always criticized and doubted new concepts and ideas in the past.

And the same is the case with bitcoin and alternative crypto-currencies.

The undeniable fact is that bitcoin is here to stay and will continue to improve to the point that it overcomes all major obstacles becoming the prime global currency for exchange of goods and services.

CHAPTER THREE

BITCOIN MINING TECHNOLOGY

3.1 Introduction

When you delve into the world of the digital currency, you are sure to encounter the terminology, bitcoin mining. This central process is essential for the creation of the digital currencies and enabling the currency to be utilized worldwide. It isn't necessary for a person to understand the process of bitcoin mining to be able to buy or spend the acquired digital currency. However, it is essential to keep in mind that "mining" is the way the digital currencies are generated with the exchange of physical cash. Even though the bitcoin mining process is technical, this esoteric technology can be comprehended by a novice.

As you already know that the distinctive feature of the digital bitcoin is that unlike paper money that is printed by the governments and is regulated by the central banks, the bitcoin is not printed. The so-called digital money is "mined" —in colloquial terms it can simply be stated that it is "discovered". In this section, we will deal with understanding the concepts of bitcoin mining, the technology that is used for bitcoin mining, and the different possibilities that bitcoin miners have so that they can make the most of the digital currencies.

Are you interested in finding out how the bitcoin money goes into circulation and how new bitcoins are released? Well, let's explore the infinite and interesting world of bit mining.

3.2   Mining Process

Before we probe further into the technology revolving around the bitcoin mining, it is essential to comprehend the basic nature of a bitcoin. Bitcoin exists only in the lines of computer programming code. Quite unlike the tangible paper currency, the bitcoin currency only subsists in a digital environment. But, this raises complex questions — for instance, "How do I generate money and more importantly without the central banks, how do bitcoins get into circulation?" All of this is accomplished by bitcoin mining.

What's Bitcoin Mining?

As people are constantly exchanging bitcoins there has to be a public ledger that is capable of maintaining the record of the financial transactions so that they can be tracked. Bitcoin mining can be described as the process of generating new bitcoins and verifying the past transactions to a bitcoin ledger, which is known as a "blockchain" in technical jargon. This distributed ledger maintains a record of all the transactions that have already take place. The blockchain consists of "blocks" and it is the miners who confirm these digital transactions so that they can be written on the ledger.

Purpose of Bitcoin Mining

The bitcoin mining has two main purposes:

a)   Create or issue new bitcoins in a block; and

b)   Verify the transactions in a secure way (without tampering) when the computational power is devoted to the respective block.

Working of Bitcoin Mining

Make a Hash

The miners enter the picture in order to provide a secure way for the transactions to take place to uphold the integrity of the blockchains. Therefore, whenever there is a block of transactions created, the miners have to put this block through a computational process. The obtained information is transformed into randomly sequenced alphanumeric characters, which are called "hash". This is done by applying a mathematical formula to the information. The hash is also stored within the block —initially, at the conclusion of the blockchain.

The hash is quite interesting — while it may appear that the creation of hash from the information (block) is simple, it modifies the facade of a block and you cannot determine what the actual data was just by looking at it. Every single hash that is created is distinct. If someone changes a single character of the bitcoin, the hash would change. By now you must be wondering whether the transactions are the only parameters involved that are used to create a hash. Well, when the miners run the process of hash generation, other data, such as, the last block's hash in a block chain is also utilized.

Why is the process of bitcoin mining so secure? The uniqueness of each hash, the dependence on the previous block's hash for the creation of a new hash for a different transaction, and the fact that even a minor tampering with the transaction will completely alter the hash all contribute in making a secure network. The bitcoin mining process ensures that the entire procedure is legitimate — everyone will figure out if anyone tries to tamper with a transaction that is already stored in a blockchain. Simply by running a hash function, you can discover whether the transactions are legitimate or fake. The blockchain technology's superior function — the preceding block's hash to create the next hash continues throughout the blocks down the chain to create a tamper-resistance and the bitcoins that have already been used elsewhere cannot be used again. This is called "sealing a block" is done by the miners.

Compete for Coins

The miners compete against one another to mine the blocks by making use of the software that is specially written for the purpose of sealing the blocks. Each time a miner creates a hash successfully, a reward of 25 bitcoins is awarded and the blockchain gets updated. All the miners on the network are alerted about the update.

The reward feature is the main reason why the miners actively keep on mining and enable the transactions to run. Apart from the bounty of 25 bitcoins, the miners are also given a fee, which is paid by the users who are sending the transactions. This fee also acts as an incentive for the miners to include the particular transaction in their respective block.

The underlying problem with this is that the creation of hash is relatively an easy process. Therefore, the miners must be presented with a complexity level so that the resource incentive process of bitcoin mining is not easy to accomplish.

The complexity level is increased to keep a steady flow of block discovery. The speed of discovery of block for creating hash needs to be regulated so that the bitcoins do not get devalued, which can easily happen if the miners are able to hash hundreds of blocks of transactions in a second. If this is not impeded, all the bitcoins will be hashed within a matter of minutes. The increased level of complexity is attained by introducing the feature in the bitcoin protocol known as proof of work (PoW). The method of PoW ensures that the new block required both time and exertion to create at the expense of processing power. The processing power requires a hardware, computational time, and energy.

The protocol of bitcoin makes it impossible to accept an old hash — the block needs to have a certain number of zeros in the beginning so that the hash has a typical appearance but until a hash is produced, one cannot truly determine what the hash will end up looking like and when you add new data, the hash will change.

The miners need to make use of new data so that they can create a different hash, which is done by utilizing another important piece of data called "nonce". The nonce is updated if the hash doesn't have a desired format — the changed value is incremented for another attempt. The whole transaction will have to be hashed again — this is what makes all the miners on a network compete as the others are also trying to uncover a workable nonce. The nonce is simply a randomly generated number. The nonce and the data in a block with the help of a hash function a hash is yielded on the mining software. The hash is a very long hexadecimal number. This means that alphabets A through F will also be a part of the hash. The difficulty target of the block is set — to be able to generate a valid block, the miner has to create a hash that will be "below" a particular set target.

In bitcoin mining, hashcash proof of work is used to generate a block. The difficulty target of the block is adjusted to ensure that it takes at least 10 minutes for a network to generate a new block. For a block discovered by the miner to get accepted on the network blockchain, the miners have to complete the proof of work that has to encompass all the data in a particular block.

The success rate is extremely low —therefore, the unpredictability factor for a processing computer to generate a block that is below a particular target increases. Since every new block contains the hash of the previous block, the blockchain requires immense work. The scheme used by bitcoin mining for proof of work is based upon SHA-256. There are other algorithms too through which the proof of work can be done. A couple of rounds of SHA 256 protocol are run on the block header. The hashing algorithm necessitates the following parameters:

A service string (hexadecimal number);

Counter; and

Nonce, which is a 32-bit number starting with 0

Bitcoin protocols are designed in a way that the difficulty target is changed after every 2016 blocks. This approximates to a couple of weeks. The readjustment of the difficulty target is automated into the protocol in order to maintain the speed of the block discovery. Look at it this way — with more computational power, the difficulty target will be increased to make it harder for the miners to identify a hash. Conversely, if the computational power decreases, the difficulty target becomes easier for bitcoin mining. With the increased number of miners, the profitability factor for each individual participant decreases. As the miners increase, each one will get a smaller share of the total payout composed of the bitcoin price, reward for the blocks and the fees paid by the people mining.

We can summarize that the bitcoin mining is a peer to peer network. The bitcoins are exchanged with the miner for solving a mathematical problem — discovering the hash for a block. The miners have to use of special software to solve this complex math problem. This way the currency is generated and more people get the incentive to participate in bitcoin mining. The miners are also required to approve the transactions. The greater the number of miner, the more secure the network is. The following process flow will make the complexity of bitcoin mining concept simpler to understand.

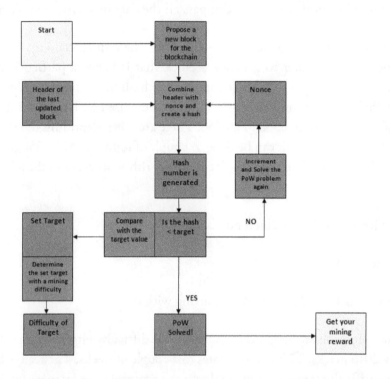

Figure 1: Flow Chart for the Proof of Work to Solve a Transaction Block

Why Is the Process Called Mining?

The process is called mining because it is analogous to the process of physical mining of precious metals and ores. Bitcoin generation is comparable to the mining of commodities because the process requires exertion and consumes energy.

The rate at which the bitcoins are generated is similar to the rate of extraction of silver and gold from actual mines in the ground.

3.3   Technology behind Bitcoin

It is evident that the bitcoin mining requires some sort of a software and hardware so that the digital currency can be raise. In this section, we will make use of the theoretical knowledge that we have gained and understand how the practical implementation of bitcoin mining is done.

How to Choose the Hardware

Before moving on to explain the bitcoin software, it is essential that a bitcoin mining hardware is chosen. This requires careful deliberation but there are two things that need to be given a priority — the hash rate and the energy consumed by the hardware.

Rate of Hashing

The hash rate is defined as the number of calculations that can be computed by the hardware in order to find a solution to the PoW problem explained earlier. There are several units of measurement for the hash rate:

Tera hashes/sec, Giga hashes/sec, and Mega hashes/sec. The rate of solving the mathematical problem of a block of transaction is directly proportional to the rate of hashing.

Energy Consumed by the Hardware

The computation requires energy, which obviously comes at the expense of money. Therefore, it is essential that you examine the power consumption in watts when the hardware is being selected. It would be frustrating to spend the earned bitcoins as a mining reward on electricity bills. Dividing the rate of hashing with the watts will reveal how many hashes you will be able to generate in a second.

Bitcoin Mining Hardware

Previously, the mathematical problems for bitcoin mining were done with the help of processors of the computers. Later on, it was discovered that the gaming graphics cars were well suited for solving mining problems as they are faster.

The graphics cards also use more electricity — as a consequence, the heat generation was also great. This made it imperative that a customized solution for bitcoin mining is suggested. This required the production of commercial products specifically programmed and redesigned for bitcoin mining. The customized chips designed were faster but still power hungry and required a more energy efficient solution. Let's explore the hardware that is needed for mining bitcoins and discover which amongst them provides the most optimized solution.

GPUs

The graphical processing units (GPUs) enhance the hash rate as opposed to the processor of the computer. They have a faster processing and can solve the transaction block problems with the SHA 256 algorithms. The ability of the GPUs to perform repetitive logical and mathematical tasks makes them more suitable for bitcoin mining.

The arithmetic logical units inside a GPU are far greater than a CPU, which is why the hashing rate is significantly greater. There are two purveyors from where you can procure GPUs: **AMD and Nvidia GPUs**. It is generally preferable to perform the bitcoin mining with AMD graphics card because the number of instructions to execute the SHA 256 algorithm on AMD is lesser as opposed to the Nvidia graphics card. Therefore, the AMD GPUs have a performance edge. Even though GPUs are still being used today for bitcoin mining, its usage is declining because of the development of faster technology.

FPGAs

FPGAs are short forms of Field Programmable Gate Arrays. These are integrated chips that can be configured by the user after manufacturing as depicted by the name. This feature of the FPGAs enables the bitcoin hardware manufacturer to procure the chips in a bulk and then customize them for bitcoin mining. The chips can then be inserted into the bitcoin hardware.

The customization benefits the miners in terms of the improvements in the performance — the FPGAs are faster than the GPUs and obviously, the CPUs. It is possible to pack more than a single GFPGA chip in a bitcoin mining hardware. The more high-end a bitcoin mining hardware is the faster the computational skills are.

ASICs

Application Specific Integrated Circuits (ASICs) were specifically designed to handle the bitcoin mining problems. The very first of the ASICs were released in the year 2013. Since then, there are versions being released in the market that have an enhanced functionality. The development of the ASICs is making other forms of hardware obsolete because of the tough competitive bitcoin mining environment.

Today, even the earlier versions of the ASICs will not be able to generate enough revenue in terms of the bitcoin currency that would exceed the exorbitant amounts of electricity bills because of excessive power consumption.

With the advent of the ASICs, more miners can participate in the process if "discovering the bitcoins". Another thing that you should be aware of is that there a "Political hierarchy" associated with the mining of bitcoins through which a miner can control the voting system of the bitcoin ecosystem. The political power bestows a miner with the power to vote for accepting or rejecting the changes bitcoin mining protocols. Nowadays, the ASIC chips can yield hashing rate in Tera hashes/ sec.

Profitability of Bitcoin Mining

To make profit from mining the crypto-currencies, you need to optimize on the rate of return of your investment. There are online mining profitability calculators available online that you can use to calculate the profitability. These web-based calculators ask you to insert information like the rate of hashing, the power consumption, the current rates of bitcoins, and the cost of the equipment.

All of these parameters are considered before estimating the time it will require you to convert the investment into a profit. Now that we have discussed the importance of the profitability and the necessary hardware, let's now discuss the second part of the bitcoin technology—the software.

Bitcoin Mining Software

The miners have to use special software in order to generate revenue in bitcoins. The software is used to solve the complex mathematical problems while the hardware runs the actual process of mining. The software instructs the hardware to execute the statements. The software also connects miners to the blockchain across the network. The best part about the bitcoin mining software is that it can be run on any operating system.

Whether it is Linux, OSX, or Windows, the software can be run. In fact, the mining software can also be run on Raspberry Pi as well. However, you will need additional drivers for the software to run on it. On FPGAs and GPUs, the software needs to be installed on a host computer that manages the bitcoin client and also the software.

Apart from relaying the input and outputs to the blockchain, the bitcoin mining software also performs some other general monitoring tasks. The mining software also monitors different statistics of the hardware, such as the speed of the fan, the rate of hashing, temperature of the hardware, and the average speed of the mining device.

There is numerous bitcoin mining software in the market — each one having its own shortcomings and advantages.

Bitcoin Mining Applications and Software for Different Operating Systems

MinePeon, EasyMiner, 50Miner, CPUMiner, and Ufasoft Miner are some the renowned Windows miners. For Mac OSX, MinePeon and EasyMiner are the best miners.RPC miner and DiaboloMiner are also some of the popular Mac OSX miners.

ASIC Bitcoin Miners

Nowadays, the manufacturers of bitcoin devices are supplying miners that have an embedded software so the miner only has to plug and play. However, in most situations, there is additional software required. BFGMIner, written in the C-language and CGMiner are some of the software that can be downloaded on ASIC bitcoin miners. Both of these are compatible with GPUs and CPUs (having different operating systems).

Free bitcoin Mining Applications

There are several bitcoin mining applications that are free of cost. Mine Peon, an open source mining application, requiring WinDisk32Imager, is one such example. There are other applications like CGMiner, EasyMiner, 50Miner, BTCMiner, Poclbm, BitMoose are some of the applications that can be installed on GPU, ASIC, FPGA, GUI Windows, Linux and Android.

Bitcoin Mining Software for Cloud

You can also invest in bitcoin mining without spending money on hardware. The investment in bitcoins can also be done with the cloud. In simple terms, it taking the help from the cloud simply means that you can take the advantage of remote data centers to fulfill the power consumption requirements for processing the complex calculations.

Local bitcoin wallets and a computer will be required to execute the communications. But, it is essential to mention at this point that there are several cons alongside the benefits of using remote data centers. The profit margin will decline as the data centre operator will charge you. This also means that the operational cost involved at your end will also decrease — no additional electricity bills and no constant humming of the hardware fans. There are chances of risk or fraud with the cloud bitcoin mining. The cloud mining can be done in the following ways:

- Lease a particular amount of hashing power — this is the most common method;

- Create your own private and virtual server and install the mining software on it; and

- Lease a third-party hosted machine for bitcoin mining.

Eobot, NiceHash, and MineOnCloud are some of the bitcoin processing power service providers.

3.4 Mining Possibilities

In broad classification, the mining possibilities can be categorized into solo mining and pool mining. There are pros and cons attached to both the mining possibilities, which we shall discuss later. Let's first explore what the two terms actually means before we indulge into describing the benefits and the shortcomings associated with both.

Solo Bitcoin Mining

Just as the name suggests, the solo mining is all do-it-yourself. All the mining blocks generated will be credited to the miner's credit. Basically, the miner performs all the mining operations solely. Firstly, you will have to download software on the computer that will consume a lot of time. This software is called bitcoin client, which is an end-user application that generates the private key and deal with the payment as well. During the downloading phase, all the transactions that are a part of the bitcoin blockchain will be loaded into the system. Apart from the significant downloading time, the second hindrance that you face with solo bitcoin mining is that it is extremely slow and requires a lot of power.

Pooled Bitcoin Mining

In pooled bitcoin mining, all the miners "pool" their resources for the bitcoin client. The solutions are generated through the collective efforts of the miners in a pool. Whenever a particular pool is able to solve the problem for a transaction, the reward is generated and it is split amongst all the participants. Mining bitcoins in a pool requires exceptional internet connectivity with a bandwidth equivalent to 10MB per day. The payouts in bitcoin mining in a pool are steady, which means that the variance is reduced. However, these payouts are decreased because the pool operator charges the miners a fee.

The Bitcoin Mining Pool Options

There are various bitcoin mining pool options available to the interested miners for the Bitcoin Core also called Satoshi Client. These options are described below:

BW Pool

This pool controls approximately 7 percent of the hashing rate of the network. The user interface of this pool is Chinese so it is extremely difficult for the English-speaking miners to comprehend it.

F2 Pool

This pool is one of the largest bitcoin mining pools. It controls approximately 25 percent of the hashing rate of the network. But, just like the BW Pool, it also has a Chinese interface.

Kano CKPool

The foundations of this pool were laid in 2014 and it has approximately 3 percent of the hashing rate of the network under its control.

BitMinter

There was a time when this pool was one of the largest one on the bitcoin mining network but now it doesn't even have 1 percent of the network's hashing rate.

Eligius

This pool was created in the days when the bitcoin mining technology came into being. However, today this pools has less than 1 percent of the network's hashing rate.

Antpool

The pool is operated by one of the largest companies in China, Bitmain. Currently this pool is the largest bitcoin mining pool and controls approximately 30 percent of the network's hashing rate.

Slush Pool

It is operated by the Czech Republic based company called Satoshi Labs. This was the very first mining pool that was formed and currently it controls a hashing rate of 7 percent. This pool muses a payout system where the early shares at the start of a transaction block are given less weight as opposed to the recent ones.

BTCC

This company is also based in China. It is not just a mining pool but also provides the bitcoin exchange services to the miners. The mining pool operated by BTCC is currently in the possession of nearly 15 percent of the total hashing rate of the network.

Pros and Cons of Solo and Pooled Mining

The solo bitcoin mining is often described as a lottery. While going solo benefits the miner in a way that the reward is not split, it also implies that the chances of receiving a reward are decreased significantly. On the other hand, because of the shared resources of all the miners in a pool, the chances of solving a transaction block quicker are enhanced significantly. On the downside, the reward of the 25 bitcoins will be split. Let's look at the pros and cons in detail.

The Pros and Cons of Pool Bitcoin Mining

Cons

- The outages at the end of the pool service provider will impact the revenue generation at the end of the miners. Other downtimes can also occur, such as DOS attacks.

- The earned income is less not only because the reward is split between the miners but also because of the fees that is to be paid to the pool provider. This fee is equal to the transaction fees so you will only get your share of the reward bitcoins.

- Pools might get attacked by cybercriminals.

Pros

- The income generation is steady unlike the unanticipated lottery earnings of the solo mining.

- The long polling supplied by the pools ascertains that the income generated is at least 1 to 2 percent higher.

The Pros and Cons of Solo Bitcoin Mining

Cons

- The bitcoin revenue generated is erratic.

- Time is wasted in solo mining.

Pros

- Has a greater immunity toward the outage, which yields higher uptime.

- It is a fee-less mining possibility and for each discovered transaction block, the miner is paid the transaction fees along with the reward of 25 bitcoins.

3.5 Conclusion

Mining is one of the highlight of the digital currency. The miners work collectively to make sure that the transactions are legitimate users isn't trying to cheat the system. They receive a reward for their efforts that results in the creation of additional money. The incentive system of the crypto-currency motivates people to contribute their effort in keeping the entire system running like a well-oiled machine.

SECTION II

BIG DATA AND NETWORK EFFECT

CHAPTER ONE

Network Economics and Crypto-currencies

1.1 Introduction

Despite the advantages of crypto-currencies as compared to the fiat currency, the latest statistics show that the network of users that use the digital currency is still small.

While the demand of crypto-currency is increasing (as evidenced by growing market cap), the number of people that use the digital currency is relatively small.

This network effect serves as an big obstacle for the digital currency from achieving its true status as an alternative digital current.

The concept of network effect represents a flywheel type of situation in which the more people that use the good, the more valuable it becomes.

Many examples can be cited of how the network effects pave way for the success of a good or services. From the telephone system and automobiles to the recent innovations such as the internet and the mobile revolution, all of them have been able to gain mainstream acceptance due to the network effects.

An offshoot of the network effect is a data network effect, which is generally not very well understood and that would be the subject matter of this chapter.

Data network effect results when the project that is powered by machine learning becomes successful when more data is obtained from the contributors.

The data network effect is very relevant to the crypto-currencies in that their entire network depends on the contribution of not just the miners and the exchanges that offer the crypto-currency but also the general public that use the currency.

The people that use the currency, the more data will be generated. And the more data that is generated the greater will be the need to incorporate core performance improvements. In short, it's similar to the economies of scale in the manufacturing sector where the more products are manufactured the greater will be the cost efficiencies. And as such, the data network effect can also be termed as data network economies.

1.2   Data Network Economics and Crypto-currencies

Data network economies in the context of crypto-currencies require certain level of investment. The investment should be made in making the data network as exhaustive as possible to benefit from the economies of scale.

Lower cost is not the aim of data network economies. Instead, greater acceptability of the currency is its main goal.

Google is the classic example of data network economies. The more people search, the more data they will offer. This data can be used to refine and improve the customer experience.

There are many other example of a company whose success is based on data network economies such as Amazon, Facebook, LinkedIn, and even Uber.

The data network economies are more relevant at the feature level as compared to the core business level. The features will keep getting better with growing ratio of users to data.

More data enables companies that offer the crypto-currency to constantly revamp the algorithms to make the product more secure and convenient for the users. The improved features will in turn attract more users that will result in greater success of the project.

The massive influx of data can also result in increased learning loop that will result in more personalized and improved services.

Moreover, the availability of cheaper and faster infrastructure to process large volumes of data and the machine learning will act as catalyst to the success of crypto currency.

Keep in mind that the data network effects don't just happen. They require persistent commitment from the start. In order to fully benefit from the big data and network economies, there is a need to incorporate a feedback loop into the system.

The feedback provided by the users of the currency can prove invaluable in improving the service. Without a feedback loop, the company cannot know what aspects to improve relating to the currency.

The feedback loop will provide data about the main features that can result in acceptability of product at a large scale. Is transaction anonymity even important in carrying out the trade? Should the crypto-currency value be backed by a commodity? Is the system of obtaining crypto-currency hassle free?

In short, the data network effect occurs when increased number of users contributes data that help in improving the functionality and ultimately the success of the product.

The data obtained by increased usage of the crypto currency can be analyzed by a company that can be used to fine tune the offering for the benefit of the users.

1.3   Sustainability of a Cryptocurrency Network

One of the criticisms of the crypto-currencies is that it behaves more like an investment instrument as compared to a medium of exchange. In order to change this perception, and thereby bring stability to the system, there is a need for promoting the use of crypto-currency among the masses.

The sustainability of the crypto-currency network depends on the acceptability of the currency among the masses. Without the support of the public, the crypto-currency will become another fad that was born with great hype but faded into oblivion without making a big dent in the financial framework.

Apart from promoting increased usage of the digital currency as a medium of exchange, the crypto-currency network can also be sustained by using improved incentive schemes for the miners.

The mining scheme is devised in a way that the early bird catches 'all' the worms. With time, it has become increasingly difficult to mine the currency.

In order to sustain the crypto-currency network it's important to evaluate the payouts and the associated fees that are used to reward the miners.

The calculation of the share that an individual miner deserves is complex. Therefore, in order to prevent any dispute, several payout schemes have been devised by the experts.

Most of the schemes concentrate on the shares that a miner has contributed in a pool and the proof of work done to uncover a block. The various payment schemes are described below:

DGM Payment Scheme

DGM stands for Double Geometric Method. It's a hybrid tactic that helps is dissolving the risk factor of the operator. This scheme allots some of the payout portion at time of the short rounds. However, during the long rounds, the payouts are distributed again in order to normalize the payments.

PPS Payment Scheme

This scheme stands for Pay per Share and it offers an instant and guaranteed payment for every solution that is solved by a miner. The miners can withdraw the payments immediately and they are paid from the current balance. This structure offers the miners the least variance and much of the risk involved is at the operator's end. This is why the reserve of PPS payment scheme needs to have at least 10000 bitcoins to ascertain that a stroke of misfortune can be endured. Despite the popularity in the earlier days, the operators are moving towards other schemes because of the increased risk factor.

SMPPS

This stands for Shared Maximum Pay per Share has an approach that closely resembles. However, according to this scheme, the miners do not get more bitcoins than earned by the pool. There is another variant of this scheme called Equalized Shared Maximum Pay per Share (ESMPPS) that equally distributes the payments to all the miners who are a part of the pool. There is another payout system that resembles these two structures. It is called Recent Shared Maximum Pay per Share (RSMPPS). According to this system, the payout is distributed to the most recent miners.

POT

It stands for Pay on Target and it is a system that offers the highest variance depending on the difficulty of the work done by a miner as opposed to the work done by a pool.

SCORE

This is a payout system where the bitcoin reward is distributed according to the time the submission was done. This is way the later shares have a greater worth as opposed to the earlier shares, which are scored by the time. The rewards are thus calculated by the proportion as opposed to the submitted shares.

Tripplemining

The scheme knits the medium-sized pools together that do not have a fee. It distributes a percent of each discovered block of transaction. This payout scheme allows the shares of a miner to grow faster as compared to other approaches.

Administers of tripplemining bitcoin mining pool utilize a portion of the generated bitcoins when a block is discovering and add them to the jackpot. The jackpot bitcoins are awarded to the miner who discovered the block. This way e very miner gets some reward regardless of their hardware's hashing speed and power.

1.4 Conclusion

All great products and ideas have succeeded in the past because they were able to get the vote of the masses. The democratization of the technological advancements means that only those ideas will be successful that are able to gain large enough vote of the public.

The big data and the network effect can play a cardinal role in the success of the crypto-currency. The conclusion that can be derived after reading this chapter is that without the acceptability of the general public crypto-currency won't be able to achieve its true potential of becoming the de factor global currency. Crypto-currency companies and government regulators can play a big role in making sure that the digital currency gets the approval of the masses resulting in data network economies at a grand scale.

CHAPTER TWO

THE BASELINE MODEL

2.1   Market Equilibrium

The price of crypto-currencies is measured against the value of the fiat currencies. So, theoretically speaking it is similar to any other currency that is traded in the exchange market.

Unlike fiat currencies, there is no official index that quotes the crypto-currency. The digital currencies are quoted on different exchanges at different prices.

That being said, the prices quoted at the exchanges tend to be similar to each other. The price of the currency is determined similar to other fiat currencies i.e. the meeting point between supply and demand.

In this chapter, we will delve in a bit detail about the demand and supply of the digital currencies, and how the equilibrium prices can be reached.

However, before moving forward we must be on the level regarding the concept of market equilibrium.

Market equilibrium is the economic concept where the supply is equal to the demand of the product. When this point is reached, the price tends to become stable.

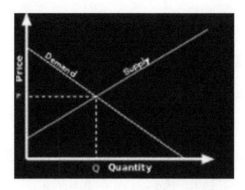

The price is below the market equilibrium when the supply is less than the demand. On the contrary, the price is above the market equilibrium when the supply is greater than the demand.

Adapting this model to the crypto-currencies, it's clear that the market equilibrium can bring stability to the prices.

The exchange value of the crypto-currencies particularly bitcoin has increased considerably after inception. At the start of 2016, bitcoin values were hovering between $700 and $1100. In contrast, at the start of the previous year the bitcoin values had hovered between $350 and $450.

The exchange values of the digital currency had appreciated by about 55 percent in 2016.

What this means is that the price of the digital currency is still searching for the market equilibrium point. The price of the digital currency has increased despite the negative publicity of the crypto-currency due to Mt. Gox collapse and other factors.

So, when will the equilibrium point be reached? And is it even possible that the equilibrium point can be achieved?

Theoretically speaking, the equilibrium point can be reached when the volume equals the consistent growth between the buyers and sellers. In other worth, when the acceptability of the bitcoin reaches to a point when there occurs a balanced growth in the demand of the currency.

Unless the digital currency is able to gain trust of the large segment of the society, its value will fluctuate at a high level. In this context, the external factors can greatly affect the supply and demand curve of the currency.

A dilemma relating to market equilibrium is that mass acceptance of the currency is required for the values to become stable and reach equilibrium levels, but the stable exchange value is required for the mass acceptance of the digital currency.

This represents a catch-22 situation that unless some external intervention is not taken can serve as an obstacle for reaching the equilibrium point for the digital currencies.

For now, bitcoin and alt crypto-currencies act more like a volatile security instead of its original goal of an alternate medium of exchange.

2.2   Demand for Bitcoin

The fluctuating value of the digital currency means that the market equilibrium has not yet been reached. Overall there has been a double digit increase in the exchange value of the crypto-currencies.

The rising value of the digital currency particularly bitcoin shows that people are slowly but surely adopting them for making the payments.

Due to being an international currency, it's not surprising that there has been an increased demand of the virtual currency in the non-western world.

Bitcoin has been seen as a refuge in Venezuela against the collapsing Bolivar. Moreover, the restrictions against capital flow in China have resulted in increasing number of people using the digital currency to transfer the funds.

The snapshot taken from Blockchain shows that the total market cap has increased considerably in the past five years.

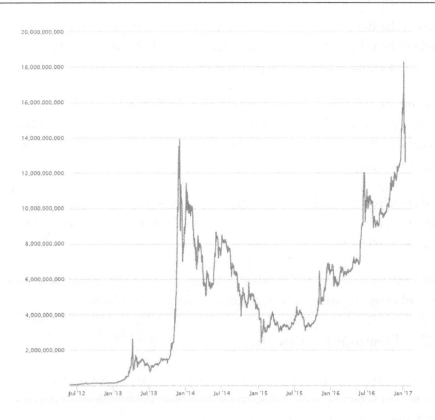

Dissecting the market volume data shows that the volume is increasing equally in both the developed and developing countries.

The snapshot at the Coin Dance website shows that the market cap of bitcoin has increased in the US from around $1.8 million in October 2013 to about $9 million in November 2016.

In the UK, the market cap has increased from half a million dollars in October 2013 to around $3 million in November 2016.

Venezuela has experienced considerable demand for bitcoin in 2016 with the market cap rising from less than $10,000 at the beginning of the year to around $731,500 by the end of the year.

The market cap in China has increased from a mere $7,500 in October 2013 to about half a million dollars by the end of 2016.

Other countries that has experienced significant increase in the demand of bitcoins include Argentina, Australia, Chile, Columbia, Czech Republic, Hungary, India, Kenya, Malaysia, Mexico, Norway, Russia, South Africa, and Sweden.

2.3 The Baseline Model

The supply of the crypto-currencies is fixed that is coded in the algorithm of the currency. The number of bitcoins, for instance is fixed at 21 million over half of which is already produced

The mechanism in which the coins are mined means that unlike the fiat currency there is no risk of hyperinflation due to oversupply of the currency.

At this point an important question arises: when would the crypto-currency value become stable? Is there any baseline model for the crypto-currency market equilibrium?

The answer is that there is no existing model that can describe the market equilibrium for the digital currency. This requires the formulation of a radical new baseline model that can predict to a certain extent market equilibrium point of the crypto currency.

To a certain extent, the modern concept of equilibrium that had been developed by Lionel W. McKenzie, Gerard Debreu and Kenneth Arrow in the 1950s can be used as a baseline model for the crypto-currencies.

The Arrow-Debreu model, for instance, is an axiomatic model of international trade. In such a model, the commodities are distinguished by when the way they are delivered as opposed to when they are delivered.

The model, in effect, represents when and under what conditions the product is delivered as well the intrinsic nature of the transaction.

A general equilibrium model can thus be made that can describe the instance when the crypto-currency value can reach the equilibrium point. Beyond that point the values will become stable and the digital currency will act more like a fiat currency.

While the baseline model that is derived from the modern equilibrium model describes the state when the values will become stable, the model in itself do not tell when exactly that state will be achieved.

The Pareto optimality – an equilibrium condition whereby it's impossible for a better position to be achieved without making at least one factor (e.g. fiat currency) worse off – can be achieved only when the price value is tied to the marginal rate of substitution.

However, the basic inference that can be made from the baseline model is that there is lack of information regarding the equilibrium value of the cryptocurrency and this can prevent us to know when the crypto-currency have achieved the Pareto optimality and thus market equilibrium.

Top of Form

2.4 Conclusion

Bitcoin and a number of other alternative crypto-currencies have been rising in value in the past few years. The increasing value represent growing depend of the digital currency.

That being said, the market cap of the digital currency is still low due to which it has not achieve a stable price. The prices are still in search of an equilibrium level. And until that market equilibrium level is not reached, the digital currencies will continue to experience wide fluctuations making them risky asset instead of a medium of exchange.

A number of obstacles are present that we had covered in the previous sections that needs to be overcome before digital currencies can be regarded as a true alternative to the fiat currencies.

SECTION III

FINANCE MARKETS AND BITCOIN REGULATION & TAXATION

CHAPTER ONE

LEGAL ISSUES IN CRYPTO-CURRENCY

1.1 Introduction

The legal issue of crypto-currency is a matter of debate in different countries around the world. The unclear nature of most legislative bodies on digital currencies makes it difficult to identify the way these currencies should be legally idealized and presented as important alternative payment arrangements. While some countries allow the use of different crypto-currencies, there are others that simply refuse to include these payment models in their transaction systems.

The time is ripe for the arrival of virtual currencies, which use distributed ledger technologies. This method allows for secure transactions and also ensures that no duplication of financial tokens is also possible during transfers that are occurring around the world. The central registry is not required in this case however, and this makes it difficult to create a legislative model as a centralized mode of financial transaction. The peer to peer exchange mechanism of virtual currencies makes it difficult to use the existing laws in order to govern the crypto-currency schemes that are currently in use.

Currencies such as bitcoin and others face legal implications in different countries, and this chapter aims to look at the different problems that are legally hampering the use of crypto-currency. The discussion especially compares the way the same digital currency is legal, as well as banned according to the different laws in a country. There is also a regulatory movement around the world in order to ensure that crypto-currency can be properly regulated in a global manner.

1.2   Legality versus Illegal

Crypto-currency generally does not cater to the traditional definition of a currency or money. A currency can be defined as a legal tool which allows sovereign bodies, such as countries to issue promissory coins and banknotes. Another important concept in this regard is that money used in a region is supposed to be centrally controlled by a state using a monetary system with strict regulations. This is not possible when using crypto-currencies that are based on distributed ledger technologies. Most virtual currencies are issued by private organizations and do not allow a single state to perform strict regulatory actions. This makes these currencies directly controlled by the market forces, which is not ideal in the case of running a strict financial model.

Another problem with currencies, such as bitcoin is the ability to work as a monetary instrument. As these currencies are not always able to fulfill the conditions of a legal tender which are different in most regions of the world, the concept of a regular system fails to legalize these crypto-currencies.

According to European Commission, a legal tender relies on three main elements. The first is that it should be backed by the acceptance of issued banknotes and coins. The second is that it should be able to offer the complete face value. The third is that it should allow a holder to discharge debt.

The United States Law for virtual currency identifies and governs the virtual currency, which is available in the country. The regulations consist of controlling the mechanisms that apply to buyers and sellers of virtual currency. This law also governs the way these digital currencies need to maintain their transparency during transactions that occur on a routine basis.

The United States Treasury officially classified bitcoin as a decentralized crypto-currency in 2013 and in fact, even the CFTC (Commodity Futures Trading Commission) classified it as a separate commodity in 2015. This allows people to speculate and sell futures regarding the currency just as they do so with the actual currencies. A federal judge also ruled in 2016 that bitcoin represents funds and are clearly definable through this term.

The US Securities and Exchange Commission (SEC) looked at stock exchanges that used bitcoin as a dominating currency, in order to find the trading of unregistered and risky securities, especially in the online world. The commission found that many websites were using illegal securities in and this regard and fined a few websites that were targeting bitcoin users to participate in fraudulent schemes.

There was a legislative draft in the State of California in 2014 that aimed to legalize different crypto-currencies including bitcoin. The consumer bureau however advised people that it was too risky to use bitcoin and other digital currencies, as investment avenues. The New York State is currently the only one that has a strong rule on bitcoin in the form of what is known as a BitLicense. There are now regulations that cover virtual currency here.

All businesses would need to give out transaction receipts and also create a policy to handle the complaints of customers under these rules. They also have to implement methods of cyber security, as well as keep a compliance officer for assuring that customers are protected against money laundering issues. There are still arguments about the legal nature of crypto-currency, such as bitcoin as there is a need for treating the different digital options in a transparent manner.

1.3 Global Regulatory Movement

According to the IMF, virtual currencies are currently considered as risky and can work as a mechanism for performing money laundering or funding terrorist activities. It is a method that can be seen as illegal in many countries, because it leads to tax evasion and encourages people who are looking to perform fraudulent activities.

It is difficult to manage virtual currencies globally, because most of them, such as bitcoin are able to affect business activities uniquely on the national levels. The impact of crypto-currency depends on the level of technological prowess in a country and the use of digital services in the field of finance.

1.4   Conclusion

Due to the confusion about the crypto-currency being an actual currency or a marketable commodity, it can be difficult to ascertain the legal nature of crypto-currency. Most countries are in the process of creating laws and regulations for crypto-currencies, such as bitcoin.

Currently, it is very challenging to regulate virtual currencies. Most crypto-currency schemes can use multiple payment systems and attach themselves to a variety of traditional currencies. This makes it difficult to evaluate them in a statistical manner and makes it difficult to carry out legal regulation of the available methods.

One of the most difficult challenges in this manner is to point out the relevant authority which should regulate them in a country let alone globally. This means that the regulation of crypto-currency throws out unique challenges that can only be resolved through the creation of new regulating bodies and legislations for virtual currencies.

CHAPTER TWO

How to Tax Bitcoin

2.1 Introduction

Crypto-currency schemes are usually opaque and decentralized, and therefore it is quite difficult to create a model of taxation for them. In most countries that legalize them as wealth assets, generally declare them as personal assets rather than treating them as individual tools of monetary exchange, such as traditional currencies. Their international nature makes it quite difficult to create a taxation model for them that can work under all the conditions.

There are different bodies that are dealing with crypto-currencies and these are the most important ones in terms of creating important taxation plans on financial objects, such as bitcoin. Most countries find that it is easier to ban crypto-currency schemes altogether, instead of creating difficult models for taxation. However, it is essential to perform taxation on these instruments and implement them as parts of the digital monetary makeup present in the modern world.

The FEC (Federal Election Commission) also had to go through the need for legalizing bitcoin as a currency, because of politicians who may want to receive donations in the denomination of bitcoins. The commission declared that such payments could not be associated as a separate currency and rather came in the definition of a valuable item when given as a donation.

The Internal Revenue Service (IRS) explains virtual or crypto currencies as the ones that present monetary value in a digital manner, and provide a medium which can be used to exchange resources. It also stresses that these currencies, such as bitcoin are available in terms of a legal tender in the country.

These digital currencies have a great potential for use in tax evasion methods. The use of a crypto-currency does not have to give away personal identity during a transaction to a governing authority. This generates the potential for carrying out transaction activities secretly. The purpose of these transactions can easily be tax evasion as a currency, such as bitcoin may not be well recognized as a financial instrument.

A crypto-currency on the other hand is able to carry out all the activities that are associated with a traditional currency such as the ability to be delivered as a payment, when buying goods from different businesses. The businesses can then use the same digital tokens to pay off their multinational employees, and avoid the liabilities that may fall on them if they use a conventional model of running a local business, and paying the employees in a locally recognized currency.

2.2   Characteristic and Nature of Bitcoin

Bitcoin is a digital currency, which can also be termed as a crypto-currency. It is a viable mode of transaction, because it can be used for payments and is accepted at multiple avenues, especially online avenues. But the actual property which can be presented as the main characteristic of bitcoin is that it is a decentralized currency, which uses a distributed ledger for carrying out financial activities across the world.

The ledger represents a financial record which is updated each time a transaction is performed. This way, the record on each ledger is updated every time that a financial transaction is performed. This ensures that a single digital payment cannot be charged twice and people can easily transfer different sums of money to one another in a secure manner. The dynamic nature of this currency on the other hand makes it difficult to follow a particular regulatory model and ensure that taxation can be readily performed in trades, wealth holdings and other activities carried out in a crypto-currency.

One issue that lies with bitcoin is that it is difficult to characterize it as either a property or a currency. It carries the special properties of both groups, and therefore poses a unique challenge in terms of using the actual regulatory strategies against it. If crypto-currency is declared as a property, then it needs to be treated locally based on the jurisdiction in which it lies. It works as a capital asset in this regard and its actual value is open to speculation, just as it is possible to do with any marketable commodity.

The crypto-currency is treated as an actual currency, and then it needs to be a tradable commodity at different exchanges around the world. It will then need to be recognized as having variable value which depends on different factors, such as those that regularly affect the traditional monetary currencies that are used all around the world.

These currencies will be recognized as objects that can be obtained through mining in order to carry out effective tax treatment when they are treated as traditional currencies. Bitcoin in this regard can be controlled in terms of putting sales tax on its transactions and obtaining a value-added tax as it is a commodity that can provide added benefits to the users and purchasers. The issue is that is important to create a consistent model that can be used around the world.

2.3   Income Tax

The United States GAO (Government Accountability Office) recommended the IRS in 2013 to properly create taxation regulations in order to control and govern bitcoin business activities. The IRS understood the need for taxing the new crypto-currency model, and has now presented a guideline for implementing federal taxes on virtual currency funds. According to the IRS, crypto-currencies such as bitcoin can be presented as holding trading or business value, which should be treated as self-employed, when looking to analyze funds for taxation requirements.

It can be difficult to implement an income tax on the bitcoins that are mined by a person or even by an organization. However, income tax applies on all kinds of payments that you receive against your services or tangible property. This means that in most jurisdictions, you have to legally report your bitcoins as income on which you are willing to pay taxes. The taxation authorities currently do not have the means to catch you for a few bitcoin transactions, but it is not advised to avoid these records from the IRS.

In most cases, the current ruling is that bitcoins should be a subject to self-employment tax. On the other hand, it is possible in some states to record the income that you have made with your bitcoin transactions, but you have to pay capital gains tax on your gains.

There are assumptions when discussing the income tax that you may have to pay on the money earned through bitcoin transactions. One of them is that these bitcoins are treated just like any other tradable commodity, such as gold or silver. However, if they are considered as a currency or a debt item, then their value will be calculated each year and the gain will be taxed in the same manner as on your savings in dollars.

The IRS does not treat currency holdings as a long-term investment and is bound to perform taxation on it each year. Bitcoin will be treated as a foreign currency by the IRS and will be included among all your other currencies when calculated for taxation.

2.4   Consumption Tax

There is a consumption tax on bitcoin in different countries, such as Japan. There is an eight percent tax in this regard which literally makes bitcoin unattractive to use in Japan. The country is now looking to abolish this high rate of sales tax on the product and finally looking to embrace the technological advancements.

One needs to remember that unlike income tax, sales tax is charged on the product each time it exchanges hands. This means that it is very difficult to quickly move a commodity through several hands when you have to pay a hefty tax on each level of the transaction.

2.5   National Approaches

The IRS currently faces a lot of problems when trying to create efficient taxation approaches for dealing with bitcoin in terms of taxation. Crypto-currencies are very difficult to perform taxation as they float on the limits of both traditional currencies and commodities.

Currently, the US government is treating all virtual currencies as properties according to the Notice 2014-21. This means that taxpayers are responsible for keeping the records of their transactions in order to pay the right amount of tax. As the different bitcoins have different values due to a volatile structure, it can be extremely difficult to find the value of the individual transactions

2.6   Conclusion

The natural tendency of bitcoin is the function as a currency or property that requires voluntary tax returns. It is difficult to ideally create a policy for taxing a quantity that changes continuously with respect to each transaction and does not hold a tangible value as an actual property would. The current taxation policies usually treat different bitcoins as coming from particular mining pools and then treat them as holding specific values just like foreign currencies.

SECTION IV

FINANCIAL INNOVATION AND INTERNET OF MONEY

CHAPTER ONE

How Digital Currencies Will Cascade up to a Global Stable Currency - The Fundamental Framework for the Money of the Future

1.1 Introduction

Crypto-currencies have earned rave reviews after it was launched in 2009. The CEO of Google, Eric Schmidt, had stated digital currencies to be the 'remarkable cryptographic achievement that has enormous value'. Moreover, Microsoft founder Bill Gates had stated that crypto-currencies are the 'techno tour de force'.

The Nobel prize-winning economist named Milton Friedman had even predicted in 1999 the development of crypto-currency that, 'The one thing that's missing, but will soon be developed, is a reliable e-cash.'

The problem with fiat money is that it has not stood well the test of time. Looking at the past we can see that it's littered with examples of monetary collapse whether it's the post-WWI collapse of the Mark, the failure of the Greek drachma in 1944, the collapse of the Mexican Peso in 1994, or the recent Venezuela's currency crises that has purchased the country to a brink of collapse.

Apart from collapse of the currencies, the inherent systematic risks and vulnerabilities present due to the manipulation of the currencies by the government pose a great risk to the global stability at the financial and economic level.

Then there is the problem of relying on dollar as an international currency of exchange as well as foreign reserves. For about half a century, the dollar has been used as the most used currency in the world.

Most of the government holds a large part of the reserves in dollars. Commodities including gold and oil are priced in dollars. International business deals are also done in dollars.

However, the 2008 financial crises had highlighted how the economic problems in America and by extension the dollar can bring havoc on the world economies.

The simple fact is more people reside outside the US than inside. That's why it makes sense to create a global form of exchange.

Digital currencies such as bitcoin can insulate countries from the ills of relying too much on dollar as a global currency. Due to the independent and collaborative nature of the underlying technology, bitcoin and alternate crypto-currencies can serve as a universal online currency that can solve all the negative points of the fiat currency.

Bitcoin is based on trust between a group of people located in different parts of the world. The transactions are conducted in a convenient and cost effective manner without any control of any single government or regulatory authority.

One prominent benefit of the digital currency as a global currency is that it can greatly reduce the cost of transferring funds from one place to another.

Bitcoin can help in remitting the money within minutes and at a fraction of the cost of transferring the funds through conventional manner. The digital currency transfers the money from one country to another thorough the internet. There is no need of the banks or other middleman when transferring the funds using bitcoins.

The experts are divided as to the possibility of the digital currency as a global currency. Some of them stress the positive aspect of the virtual currency with great potential, while others argue that crypto-currencies behave more like an investment option instead of a currency.

The status of digital currency is different all over the world. In majority of the countries, the crypto-currencies are not illegal, but they are unregulated. Since the bitcoins do not violate a legal framework, the countries don't have sensible justification for shutting down the virtual currency.

Moreover, the reason that the digital currency has not been completely outlaws is that they represent a completely transparent global currency secured by cryptography.

In other words, the crypto-currencies are seen as a positive alternative to the traditional fiat currency.

The digital currency bypasses the traditional method of transfer of funds. The transaction does not involve payment of fees to financial middlemen that results in a great cost savings. It is due to the same benefit that merchants all over the world are starting to accept bitcoin payments despite the issues with the digital currency that we had covered in previous chapters.

Bitcoin payment processors such as BitPay make it easier for individuals to make payments online. The payment processor has got the support of one of the most visible retailer in the global online community – WordPress.

Since other payment options such as PayPal are not supported in a number of countries, bitcoins serve as a perfect alternative global currency.

The distinguishing feature of digital currency that differentiates it from the fiat currency is that the supply is not controlled by any central bank. Instead, the algorithm of the virtual currency has fixed the supply of the currency.

Being an independent currency, no country can lay claim over the digital currency. This prevents the risks of a currency collapse due to overprinting of currency.

Bitcoins do not have any physical representation. They are not printed like a fiat currency. Instead they are stored on electronic devices such as smart phone, laptop, or PC. This makes them convenient for online transfer of funds.

The crypto-currency can be spent on both the goods and services. Users can conduct the transaction anonymously without any intervention from a third-party.

No central clearing house is present nor is there any intermediary institute has authority over the digital currency. They can be easily obtained, as mentioned before, by mining, exchange of fiat currency, or by offering goods and services.

People can use bitcoins to buy the goods and services anywhere in the world from merchants that accept the crypto-currency. The constantly growing number of merchants that accept the virtual currency reflects that increased acceptance as a mode of exchange.

At this point, you should realize that the virtual currency is different from the electronic currency. With electronic money, the link with traditional currency is preserved. They do not have any inherent value.

The crypto-currency, on the other hand, behaves similar to any other currency in that they have a value that is determined by the demand and supply of the currency.

Experts have two opposite views when it comes to bitcoin as a global currency. One view is that bitcoin does not serve as a currency. Instead, the virtual currency acts like a speculative instrument with large fluctuations.

The other view about crypto-currency is that it has a strong future potential as a global currency as it is independent of any control by a regulatory authority.

When used as a currency, bitcoin offers greater transparency, reduced transaction costs, and faster payment processing as compared to the traditional currency.

The transaction fees are much lower as they only cover the efforts of the miners in verifying the transactions. There are no costs linked to other parties such as the regulatory authority, storage provider, or any other third-party intermediary.

The costs of traditional currency are relatively higher as besides the costs involved in clearing the transaction, the fees are to be offset against overhead costs, transport, storage, and security costs.

The average transaction fees for transfer of fund using between is between 0 and 1 percent while for the traditional currency the fees is 2 to 5 percent or more.

Moreover, the speed of execution of bitcoin transfer is as low as 10 minutes. In contrast, it generally takes days for the transaction to be cleared in the case of international transactions.

We may thus conclude that virtual currencies can in theory serve as a perfect alternative to the fiat currency. However, while the potential of the crypto-currency as an alternate mode of payment is great, at present the framework is lacking for it to be implemented for the mass market.

Experts are of the view that there is a need for abstraction so increased disruption to take place. The foremost thing that should be addressed is the price. The price at which a bitcoin is addressed leads to capital gains or loss. This increases the complexity in accounting of the funds particularly for taxation purposes.

The solution should be to make changes in the bitcoin algorithm in order to make the price fluctuation more stable. The stability of the currency value will lead to increased confidence about the currency. It would also make it easy to calculate the amount of tax due on the funds.

In other words, there is a requirement for improvement of the bitcoin protocol and the general framework of the currency. This is a task that can be taken on both the national and the corporate level.

However, bitcoin should be considered more than just a currency. It is a mode of exchange as well as a facilitator of trade. The decentralized nature of the currency will result in global trade of goods that will no doubt boost the respective economies of the countries.

The use of crypto-currency has the potential to improve the financial services in making it more efficient and cost effective. This will translate into increased economic activities that will make a positive impact on the global economy.

From the above discussion, it is clear that bitcoin holds great potential as a digital currency. The delays in transactions can be largely eliminated while the transaction costs can be halved.

However, the digital currency has certain disadvantages at least at a commercial level. There can be no recourse in case of a fraud since the transactions are irrevocable once confirmed and entered in the public ledger.

Also, episodes such as the theft of bitcoins from Mt. Gox account should not repeat if the virtual currency is to thrive as a global currency. In the Mt. Gox case in particular several people had lost their entire life savings.

Critics say that the failure of Mt. Gox to protect people's money represented the death of the virtual currency. On the other hand, the proponents had said that the problem was caused due to internal security loopholes.

For the opponents, the case of Mt. Gox had represented all the concerns about bitcoin as a global currency: anonymous transaction, decentralized system, and lack of governmental control. Hackers had overloaded the system with fake transactions that forced the company to halt transactions and ultimately lose all the funds of the customers with no prospect of getting them back.

Supporters including rival exchange companies have stated that the blame lies solely with the management of Mt. Gox instead of the bitcoin currency. In addition, the CEO of Mt. Gox, Mark Karpeles, had also admitted to the fact that the responsibility for the loss falls on the company's own internal control, and that the crypto-currency itself cannot be blamed.

Whatever the views of the experts, the fact of the matter is that the low-control environment, anonymous transaction, and decentralized nature of the exchange expose investors to a great risk. If the digital currency is to become a global currency, framework needs to be developed that addresses the same issues.

The millions of dollars that were lost due to the Mt. Gox fiasco represents puncture in the trust bubble, which is necessary to keep a financial system afloat.

The framework of the bitcoin should be focused on security and safety of the customers' funds. Without the underlying security framework, it's possible that the bitcoin revolution will fall down like a house of cards that is placed on an unstable surface.

Experts believe that bitcoin technology is at a nascent stage. Once the crypto-currency technology has matured enough there is a great possibility of its use as a global currency.

The idea of creating a global reserve is not new at all. The analysts say that the digital currency is likely to gain greater popularity as the flaws and the security loopholes are addressed. With a solid framework, we can expect crypto-currencies such as bitcoin being increasingly used as a preferred means of transferring funds on a global scale.

Most of the countries have faced great difficulties in managing the monitory policy despite having different currencies. A unified global currency is expected to solve the problems with existing fiat currency-based exchange system instead of creating additional issues.

At the present, it's hard to imagine crypto-currency as a global currency being used for international trade. But the currency certainly has the potential to revolutionize the global financial and monetary system.

1.2 Regulatory Framework for Cryptocurrency

Looking at the future, we can say the future of the crypto-currency will be likely to be of growth. However, if the technology is to be accepted by the mainstream, the policies need to be implemented to avoid hackers and criminals from abusing the system.

The current legal framework, however, does not provide a clear protection to the fund holders. The Mt. Gox case has shown the extent to which people are exposed to loss due to theft and mismanagement of the funds. The possibility of similar trust-destroying news relating to the crypto-currency cannot be ruled out.

That being said, instead of completely banning the currency, government should devise programs to make the system free of abuse and criminal activities.

Bitcoin and other crypto-currencies are innovative open source solutions. No gatekeeper oversees the currency creation and creating them requires nothing more than device connected to the internet.

The independent nature of the eco-system is one of the main reason of its rising popularity and support. The technology helps break down the barriers to international transaction and turns the world into a true global village.

However, this very independent and open nature of the system makes it vulnerable for abuse. A number of cases have occurred of account holders losing all their money due to hackers exploiting a security flaw.

In the interest of the general public, the regulators need to monitor and regulate the crypto-currency network to avoid it being used as a vehicle of abuse.

The regulators should device rules and policies that can help in identifying the scams from the innovations. Having said, that up till now the crypto-currency has served as a rubric for the regulators.

Any policy regarding the crypto-currency should be a flexible instead of a static principle. The policy must be capable of being modified according to the needs.

Increased attention should be paid by the policymakers on schemes that are devised to offer profits to the investors. The challenge is to find out whether the federal securities law applies to the scheme.

In this respect, the Howey test can be used that has been taken from the 1946 Supreme Court case that clearly laid out the instances when a scheme is considered a contract transaction.

A contract, according to the Howey test, is a security transaction when:

- A person invests money.

- The money is invested in an enterprise

- The person experts to earn a profit

- The profit is earned due to the efforts of a third part

According to the Howey test, the contract can be considered a security irrespective of whether they are evidenced by a formal certificate or a nominal interest. The test is more flexible in determining the nature of the transaction and in searching for the meaning of a security.

In other words, the form is disregarded when determining the inherent nature of the transaction and instead the emphasis is on economic reality.

In this context, a person that purchases a crypto-currency is considered to have purchased a nominal interest in the asset.

Moreover, this opens the debate whether the crypto-currency that is offered to the public is really a currency or an unregistered security.

When it is inspected in the context of the Howey test, obtaining coins on a virtual currency network can be classified as investing in a security since the crypto-currency acts more like a security than a currency

However, additional complexity is created by the fact that while the person may purchase the currency from the network, the currency is not owned by the network. In addition, the currency does not occur in the balance sheet of the issuing company.

The record of the transaction is kept by miners or validators instead of the issuing company that complicates the matters further. So, do the miners fit the description of the issuer of the currency or are they the promoters?

The above discussion shows that the special underling structure and working of the virtual currency makes it difficult to classify for the regulators.

The situation presented above is in favor of the argument that crypto-currency is a rubric for the regulators. It shows the difficulty for the policy makers in issues definitive laws relating to the security.

One of the suggestions that were made by the European Central Bank (ECB) was that the owners of the crypto-currency network should register is the respective jurisdiction to allow regulation and oversight. However, the problem is that there is no central owner of the virtual currency scheme. The ECB had admitted that it is difficult to regulate the crypto-currency due to its inherent working.

The attempts to get the virtual currency network firms are hampered by the fact that there are no geographical boundaries or central points of access. The servers are located in different locations that are not within the jurisdiction of a single central government.

However, the above does not mean to say that the bitcoin and alternate currencies cannot be regulated. They can be indirectly controlled through regulations for trading floors, exchanges, and other financial entities.

An example of a crypto-currency system under the regulatory framework can be given of the partnership between Paymium, bitcoin exchange, and Aqoba, a payment service provider, in France that alolows users to carry on transactions while benefiting from the protection offered by the Fonds de Garantie des Dépôts et de Résolution (FGDR) that acts similar to the Federal Deposit Insurance Corporation.

Another way the crypto-currency can be regulated is by requiring the network to avoid illegal transactions to be carried out from the website. Also, they should be required to show the personal identity or IP address of users that are suspected of money laundering or other types of illegal activities.

However, a problem with this approach is the tools to identify fraudulent activities are not fully developed that can be used by the exchanges.

The Treasury Financial Crimes Enforcement Network (FinCEN) had issued a guidance statement in 2013 for both miners and exchangers of virtual currency. The FinCEN had defined them as a money service providers or transmitters and subject to its regulations.

The policymakers need to take an aggressive approach towards criminal activities committed using the virtual currency. The US Department of Homeland Security had already demonstrated this behavior when it seized funds held at Mt. Gox by Dwolla - a payment service provider that were used by many people to transfer the funds.

The decentralized nature of the exchange system makes it open to attack by the hackers. Thanks to the anonymous nature of the transactions, identifying the victims is not an easy task at all. Not only is the process time consuming but resource intensive as well. Moreover, the growing usage of the crypto-currency will make it harder to track deviant activities.

Consider for instance, hundreds of thousands of sites similar to Silk Road all engaged in illegal activities? Exposing all the culprits in such a situation can be an impossible task.

What is required is to create a solid framework that can prevent the illegal sites that use crypto-currencies from existing in the first place. The most practical approach that the governments can take is to attempt to regulate the transactions that can take place at the crypto-currency network rather than banning the system altogether.

The crypto-currency networks should be regarded similar to the currency and commodities exchanges. Due to the great potential of the virtual currencies, it would be unwise for the government entities to take a more hostile approach towards the crypto-currency.

The government should not try to outlaw the crypto-currencies because:

- Crypto-currency offer considerable economic advantage over other method of payments

- The currencies are not illegal in themselves under the existing regulations of any country

- The government does not currently have the ability to directly target the crypto-currency network

The government should not put regulatory restrictions on the crypto-currencies is not an argument against the regulation. Instead, it means that the government should avoid stifling the innovation.

New legislations should be devised to identify the nature of the crypto-currency transactions. This can be done through close analogies to existing regulations.

Whatever happens to the crypto-currency remains to be seen. The undeniable fact is the virtual currency solves a lot of problems that plague the existing mode of payment. The US Federal Bureau of Investigation (FBI) had admitted that the crypto-currencies are being used for both legal and illegal purposes. What is required is to discourage the illegal and support the legal through a process of effective regulations and policies.

Due to the lack of any centralized authority and anonymous nature of the transactions, it's not possible to fully monitor, regulate, and report on the illegal activities. However, steps can be taken to minimize the cases of abuse of the crypto-currencies.

Under the existing anti-money laundering acts in different countries, many of the third-parties that are involved in the crypto-currency transactions are considered to be transmitter of money. That's why it's important that they register themselves and collect certain information about users that can help prevents money laundering and illegal activities.

The confusion regarding implementing legislation can be realized from the letter that was issued by the Department of Financial Institution in California making a cease and desist order to the Bitcoin Foundation.

The State of California's financial authority had failed to realize that the Foundation is only a nonprofit organization that does have any authority over sale of the virtual currency. The Foundation had made it clear in the response letter stating that even if it winds up the operations, the crypto-currency activities will continue as it does not have any control or jurisdiction over the currency.

Instead of trying to stop the operation of the crypto-currencies, the regulatory authorities should put forward rules safeguarding the interests of the public. This will be beneficial in the long run to the consumers and the community at large.

1.3   Commodity-Backed Digital Mint

The pressing problem that act as an obstacle for crypto-currencies to be adopted as a digital currency is that the extreme volatility. Like the fiat currencies, bitcoin and other alternative currencies are not backed by any commodity such as gold, silver, or oil.

As we had mentioned previously, lack of stability is the major obstacle for crypto-currency to be used as a global currency.

Some experts have put forward the idea that the commodity-backed digital currency can solve the problem of volatility to a great extent.

Instead of the demand and supply of the currency, the value of the crypto-currency should be pegged to the value of a commodity.

The commodity backing means that a certain amount of a commodity such as gold will be backing the currency. It means that the currency can be exchanged for a commodity at a particular exchange rate.

At the present the value of the crypto-currency experience, great fluctuations that make it unfeasible for the merchant to price their goods in the digital currency. But once the value of the crypto-currency stabilizes, there is chance that the merchants will quote the price directly in virtual currency.

In this way, the crypto-currency can become a truly global currency that can be used by merchants in quoting their goods. Backing the cryptocurrency to a commodity might give a competitive edge to the currency against the fiat currency, which is not backed by anything.

The commodity backed cryptocurrency would provide the benefits of the both worlds. Essentially, it can offer the convenience of faster processing of international payments and also provide the stability of a commodity value such as gold.

The crypto-currency would in other words act similar to a gold certificate but due to its inherent characteristics deemed as a substitute of the fiat currency.

Thus, the commodity backed crypto-currency would have the intrinsic value of the gold but also the portability and speed of the digital currency. This kind of crypto-currency will have a mass appeal as compared to a purely digital currency.

People are reluctant to trust a virtual currency. But if it is backed by a solid physical commodity, they would be more ready to place trust on the currency.

Looking back at the commodity prices, we see that there has been rarely extreme fluctuation in prices. The commodities do not normally experience fluctuation similar to crypto-currencies whose value changes by hundreds of dollars within a matter of days.

The commodity backed digital currencies will receive greater support from the masses as most tout stable money reform. Crypto-currency is a promising idea but lacks the tangibility that either rouses doubt or create fear.

One of the most renowned proponent of a commodity-backed crypto-currency is the Republican candidate for 2016 US presidential election, Ryal Paul. He had stated that he would like to the digital currency to be backed by a basket of commodities.

While the commodity-backed cryptocurrency may seem like the best of the both world scenario, there are certain negative impact as well.

A digital currency that is tied to a commodity will generally increase the transaction costs. This is because the system will rely on a team of miners to validate the transactions as well as personnel to calculate the value of the currency that is pegged to a digital currency. Even automated systems will have attached maintenance and capital costs. These costs will be reflected in the transaction fees charged to the customers.

1.4   Making Bitcoin Successful Through Information Cascade

Information cascading is a method that can help in getting people to use the bitcoin. One of the main deterrent of adopting digital currency is it relatively unpopularity as a mode of payment.

Only a small percentage of the global population knows procedure on how to use the bitcoin for exchange percentage. Majority of the people seem to be in the dark as to how to use the digital currency for buying and selling goods online.

The acceptability of bitcoin depends upon other factors the information available online regarding the use of the digital currency. At the moment, however, they are not used as a currency medium but as a mode of investment.

People at the present it seems are generally not interested in how the currency facilitate exchange, but how it can help in making profit in the short term. This phenomenon is known as information cascading in which the decision of one group of people directly affects the decision by the others.

As discussed in previous chapters, bitcoin fulfills the definition of a currency. However, they are considered by the public as an investment instrument due to the information cascading.

People hold this view because others also have the same view. They are in fact following a trend without knowledge of the inherent characteristic of the virtual currency.

An information cascade happens when a person acts after observing the action of others despite of contradictory information signals. The information cascade situation occurs when persons ignore the contradictory private signals and base the decision on the actions of others.

The phenomenon of information cascade can be observed in the fields of politics, financial market, and corporate sector. The information cascades when there is no direct communication with the individual. Instead, the information is communicated through the action of others.

The information cascade can be explained by a simple example.

Suppose that three individuals have to select either to accept or reject a choice. Each individual makes the choice sequentially or one after the other.

Individual A is the first person to make the choice. The selection will be made using personal information. Let's assume that the person agrees the offer.

Now the second person will base the decision based on own personal preference and also the public information about the choice made by the other person. Let's suppose for simplicity purposes that the person accepts the offer as well.

The third person is expected to ignore the personal information and make the decision based on the public information i.e. accept the offer. This will result in the creation of an information cascade. The third individual will just imitate the previous individuals in making the decision.

The information cascade does not always lead to the acceptable behavior. When the information cascade leads to a profitable decision it is said to be an up-cascade. On the other hand, if the information cascade leads to an unprofitable decision, it is said to result in a down-cascade.

The information cascade leads to a herd behavior. This happens when a large number of individuals imitate the actions of others when making the decision. The decision is made on the premise that not everyone would be wrong about a subject.

Another important aspect of the information cascade is that it is brittle or fragile by nature. The individuals act according to public observation or heresy without making any research on their part.

When actions are taken based on the private information it is known as the information externality, or an outlier, that is added to the public information.

A real-world application of the information cascade phenomena is the people making decisions based on the recommendation of the experts. Newbie investors mostly make the mistake of basing decision on public information without carrying out their own research.

The information cascade phenomena can be applied to making crypto-currencies successful. Through information cascade the digital currency can be made to be accepted by the masses.

By persuading the public to purchase crypto-currency, the financial experts can begin the information cascade process. The more the experts take part in the up-cascade of the digital currency, the greater are the chances of the currency being adopted by the large segment of the population.

The information cascade can be a powerful tool used by the proponents of the digital currency. And the fact is that the digital currency deserves the hype and support of the expert as it serves as a convenient and cost –effective medium of exchanging the funds.

1.5   Conclusion

Crypto-currencies are at the present used by a minority of people. They are mostly used outside the existing banking and regulatory framework. The online nature of the digital currency creates difficulty in regulating the exchange.

The fact is that the digital currencies are at an early stage of development. They have the potential to greatly transform the financial landscape by changing the way funds are transferred.

The digitization of the currency is taking place around the world. The digital currency should be taken seriously by financial pundits, policy makers, and also the public since it can have a beneficial effect on the nature of payments and exchanges.

The crypto-currency that was first introduced in 2009 was not the first attempt to digitize the currency. Others system had introduced in the past five decades. However, either they failed to become popular or the idea flopped the moment after introduction.

What makes the current crypto-currency revolution remarkable is that the system is the first with deep structure, trading momentum, and relatively greater adoption.

The technology of bitcoin blends easily with the existing infrastructure and communication tools. The payment medium combines the ease of using the credit cards with the cost effectiveness and anonymity of using the cash.

The merchants, government, and the public at large care what money is used for the exchange of goods. The money to be acceptable must carry a value, should be stable, and easy to transfer and store. Crypto-currency offers great benefits to the users, and once all the flaws are solved, it can replace the traditional currency as a medium of exchange.

Due to the extreme fluctuations, the currency cannot be practically used as a store of value. The value of crypto-currency is not backed by any commodity or a government. Instead, the demand of the currency results in the fluctuation in its value.

However, once a solution is devised such as a commodity backed crypto-currency mint the digital currency can become the de facto global currency. This will require a concentrated effort by both the crypto-currency service providers and the government legislators. The efforts should be focused on plugging in the security flaws and making it blend in with the existing regulatory framework particularly relating to taxation and anti-money laundering.

An independent global currency can solve the problems that occur due to the financial and credit crunch or the exchange rate fluctuations, which create a major headache for the global investors.

Due to the way that the currencies are mined, the digital currencies have a negligible rate of inflation similar to gold. Moreover, they also offer portability and transferability benefits similar to cash. But what makes the digital currency superior to both is the low transaction cost and processing time that is involved in the traditional modes of exchange.

Once all the loopholes associated with the digital currencies are closed, the cryptocurrency can be able to attract a large number of individuals that will pave way for the currency to replace the existing mode of payment.

The crypto-currency won't be subjected to extreme valuation when it is adopted at a large scale. The framework of the digital currency is built in a way that allows it to sustain itself without any outside intervention.

CHAPTER TWO

BITCOIN: A LOOK AT THE PAST AND THE FUTURE

With the origin of instantaneous communication, the rise of crypto currencies was obvious. Among 400+ types of crypto currencies, Bitcoin seems to be at least one-decade ahead of the real-time. And this declaration reflects not only the outstanding features of Bitcoin, but also the way it has took and won over its potential competitors like Apple Pay.

Today, Bitcoin is accepted by not only internet leaders like WordPress, Microsoft, Reddit, Wikipedia, The Pirate Bay, and others, but leaders from other industries have also started embracing this trendsetter of digital currencies. You can *eat fresh* at Subway, rent cars or book tickets on Cheap Air, gorge upon sushi at The Pink Cow in Tokyo, purchase organic food from Whole Foods, and even donate/deal with The Libertarian Party or State Republican Party in the US, using Bitcoin.

It takes at least 2–3 days to confirm credit card payment at a restaurant, retail store, or any other place. Bitcoin takes only 10 minutes. Speed is not its only important feature. It is also fair, transparent, and quite secure from traditional techniques of theft, including cyber-crimes.

It might seem a little deceptive to believe that digital currencies will take over the plastic, metal, and paper money, considering the current monetary systems. But, Bitcoin is a reality, just like technology, and just like you and me.

Several major institutions have adapted to the modern economic pattern and others have reserved judgments. The chances of governments adapting to crypto currencies are high. It is because the governments are interested in tracking national financial dealings and establish ways to monetize them in a way that favors national economy. We will explain it in the Role of Government section. Here, let's have a look on the risks, challenges, and chances of success of Bitcoin.

2.1   Reasons for Success and Failure

In 2013, Bitcoin's highest worth per coin was recorded as USD 1220. In February 2014, Mt. Gox, the Japanese exchange that managed around 70% of Bitcoin transactions in 2013, declared Bankruptcy. Unclear reasons and the loss of USD 390 million aroused predictable agitation among Bitcoin users. In January 2016, the worth of one Bitcoin was USD 380.

Bitcoin was never a total failure. Since arrival, it has worked like any ordinary currency with fluctuations in market value. A majority of the Bitcoin investors believe that one Bitcoin will hit the rate of USD 1million+. An evaluation of the reasons of its success and failure can help create policies for future implementation.

Reasons of Failure

Mt. Gox theft crime led to the downfall of Bitcoin, although the crypto currency is rehabilitating its financial value. Mt. Gox was opened in 2010 for trading playing cards. Magic: The Gathering Online eXchange or Mt. Gox is an obsessive game, specifically designed for school-going kids, who have lost the hope of becoming cool. After the arrival of Bitcoins, the company started Bitcoin exchange and gave up on the cards. In 2013, Bitcoin hit its highest per-coin value. In February 2014, Mt. Gox declared bankruptcy, a loss of USD 450 million at that time.

Mt. Gox did not provide any authentic reason for the loss. However, interrogations revealed that the coins were stolen from Mt. Gox's hot wallet. The process of theft started in late 2011, according to the interrogations. In June 2013, the withdrawal was suspended. Legal interrogations are still in process. What could have caused the failure? Irrevocable Money! Aside this primary reason of failure, we will also discuss some other reasons here.

- ## Irrevocable Money

Unlike traditional currency, the crypto currencies are irrevocable. A buyer cannot reverse the payment, like in hand-to-hand cash payment. This feature is unsuitable for the person who pays i.e. buyer and suitable for the person who gets money i.e. the seller. The coins can be returned on court orders only, the decision of which is unpredictable after proceeding the case. Similar strategy was used in Mt. Gox's case.

- ## Reduced Processing Speed

Mike Hearn was a high-profile Bitcoin developer. The long-time proponent withdrew all Bitcoin investments in January 2016. Mike did not provide any specific reason for withdrawal. The reduced processing speed of transaction could be one of the reasons. Bitcoin works as block-chains. As the transactions continue to increase, the size of blocks in a chain also increases. This leads to slow processing speed of a transaction. In long-term, if Bitcoin takes over the fate currency, the size of blocks will multiply with number of global population using Bitcoin. The speed will continue to decrease, if a serious and careful action is not taken.

- ## Absence of an Intermediary

While the absence of an intermediary is a positive feature, at the same time, it is a drawback, especially when a crime occurs. The coins are stored in user's wallet. Phishing, network hacking, system failure, or any kind of advance cyber-crime may lead to losing all investment. An intermediary authority is responsible for devising laws and policies against money laundering, cyber-crime, and other financial crimes. Furthermore, the insurance companies do not offer insurance for Bitcoins, which simply means that the chances of recovering Bitcoin investment are null.

Reasons of Success

WordPress became the world's first company to accept Bitcoin payments in 2012. Since then, Bitcoin has been widely accepted in different industrial and commercial sectors. In 2013, its net market value exceeded USD10 billion. In the same year, Genesis manufactured the first Bitcoin ATM in Vancouver.

At consumer level, the largest benefit of using Bitcoin is the reduced cost. At business level, the benefits are many. Let's have a look on the factors that contributed to the success of Bitcoin, and that have made it survive even after a fatal loss.

- **Greater Liquidity**

Bitcoin boasts the world's largest network in crypto-currencies. Due to its greater liquidity, the approach of converting Bitcoin into fiat currencies is easier, and more profitable. If Bitcoin continues to grow at the same pace, chances are that the value of one Bitcoin will increase unexpectedly; USD 1 million is the prospective value.

- **Payment Freedom**

Unlike bank transactions, Bitcoin does not have high fees per transaction. Aside processing fee, it does not have taxes on transactions, which makes Bitcoin a suitable choice for businesses.

- **Anonymity**

When two parties process, a transaction using Bitcoin, the public address can be seen by other Bitcoin users. However, the identity of both parties remains anonymous. The anonymity of identity is one of the most profitable benefits, especially for the businesses who want to escape high state and federal taxes.

- **Speedy International and Long-Distance Transactions**

The transfer of a certain amount from one American state to another takes around 3–5 days. When a customer swipes the credit card on restaurant's credit card machine, the transaction is processed through multiple institutes and confirmed in around three days. Some international transactions take longer. In Bitcoin transaction, the parties exchange QR Codes. The internet protocol processes the transaction within 10 minutes, and the process completes. Bitcoin has sped up international and long-distance transactions, compressing the process from days to minutes.

2.2 A Numismatic Approach

Satoshi Nakamoto created Bitcoin in 2009. It was created for mysterious market, which is still unknown. The idea behind Bitcoin was to create a channel of money exchange for goods or other currencies without using traditional banks. Cheap online payments, fast processing, easy access, and no fee processes were some reasons that created the Bitcoin hype.

2013 was the lucky year for Bitcoin. Its popularity decreased after the Mt. Gox scam. The currency regained its value in 2015. The value continued to increase in 2016. In January 2016, the value of one Bitcoin was USD 538. The June 2016 report reveals that Bitcoin ATMs constitute to 24% global market share.

Business Perspective

Bitcoin has the benefit of securing the business transactions. It gives an opportunity of tax-free exchange of value to the businesses. The anonymity feature provides identity protection to the businessmen.

The currency investors use Bitcoin to maximize their profits. Since 2009, Bitcoin has proved to be a profitable currency investment resource for businesses, expect that of 2013.

2.3 The End of Money

The proponents of Bitcoin believe it to have the potential to completely replace the fiat currency. The role of governments, international relations among countries, and ruling elites cannot be neglected in this regard. Complete replacement of banking system means uncontrollable friction among the economies. The global economics will fall down, if not crash, for some time.

However, the perception of Bitcoin as a source of ending money is backed by certain reasons. Firstly, Bitcoin has revealed its strength in 2013. Had the Mt. Gox theft not happened, Bitcoin would have continued growing, putting many economical leaders to shame. It has already reached critical mass. The network is expanding its wings on global skies.

An undeniable factor, important to believe in the strength of Bitcoin, is the global technological assistance. When Bitcoin started, it was an idea of revolutionizing world investment systems. Today, it is backed by the technological experts from all around the world.

Bitcoin may not completely put an end to money but a sure shot is that it will be used as a global mode of currency exchange. We will see more digital currencies on the financial battleground. Countries will build their own digital currencies, just like traditional currencies. This will lead to the expansion of digital currency networks. In 10–15 years, Bitcoin and digital currencies may not end money but these will be used in routine life.

Bitcoin as Internet of Things

The arrival of internet was revolutionary and predictable. But the arrival of Internet of Things was unpredictable. Starting from email to HTTP protocol and ecommerce, several fascinating technological chapters took over the first email sent, though it still boasts its historical importance. Bitcoin may also take a similar path. Bitcoin will thrive, revealing new technological facilities on its fundamental platform. The predictable technologies include developing a protocol for digital exchange of fiat currencies, service protocols for purchasing foreign properties through banks, protocol for tokenizing assets, and many others.

2.4   The Role of the Government

Bitcoin and other digital currencies have faced devaluation and market fluctuation due to government restrictions, imposed to limit the use of Bitcoin. Several reasons explain the government restrictions, and anonymity of transactions is the most important one.

It wouldn't be exaggeration if we say that the age of digital currencies has arrived. With sped up communication systems, it will take merely a few years to witness the globalization of Bitcoin. The political parties have started to accept Bitcoin. Soon, the governments will also embrace its 'obviousness'.

The governments can establish and impose policies to regulate Bitcoin transactions. As there is no central controlling authority, the government policies will be helpful in destabilizing the possibility of criminal links that are using Bitcoin and other digital currencies for exchange of value.

• The Anonymity of Transactions

The anonymity of transactions favors the criminal activity the most. As explained earlier, the users exchange value in Bitcoin with public addresses. The value is exchanged in their Bitcoin wallets. They have private addresses too to process the transactions. People can see the public addresses of transactions/exchange of value. The government agencies can eradicate the chances of criminal activity by establishing a centralized national database, based on private addresses. It will include registration of sorts. This way, the anonymity of Bitcoin users will remain in the public. However, the transactions will be recorded in the national database.

• Cap Management

Eradication of anonymity of transactions will not be appreciated by entities from the corporate sector, which may build pressure on the governments. However, as there is no central regulatory authority, the chances of mismanagement during inflation and deflation times are high due to lack of policies. Restricted cap is one of the key factors in policy devising. Bitcoin, with market cap of 21 million coins, is supposedly unsuitable for policymaking. The government will either extend the digital currency market cap or completely remove it, like fait currency. Cap management is necessary for the governments to artificially manipulate the financial systems and money circulation.

• Security Restrictions and Cyber Control

Although Bitcoin offers greater security against identity theft, yet cases like RAT and CCSM that we have explained earlier, tend to breach the user security. The government will create certain conditions and terms to evaluate the eligibility of the crypto currency protocol. These will include security restrictions and conditions against cyber control. Security enhancement is already under consideration. Threshold cryptography i.e. the technique of breaking the protocol and distributing its parts on different storage networks like cloud and smartphone will be included. The government will also require security against loss of money due to system or network failure.

- **Currency Valuation and Friction Management**

Bitcoin is an international currency. It is not bound by geographical or regional restrictions. It has similar value all over the world. However, this feature of Bitcoin is although favorable for the public, but it is a nightmare for the governments. It also has a strong, less-understood impact on the private lives of public. Say, if a person from a high-economy zone travels to a low-economy zone, the trip will cost much lesser than the cost of a trip within the city. Aside tourism, it will also impact the labor cost of global businesses and taxation costs of import and export. Simply, put, it will have an impact on overall global economy. At grass-root level, it will reduce the friction caused due to exchange of currencies with different values. The purpose of Bitcoin may be lost if the governments impose currency valuation-based policies.

On the other hand, the involvement of the governments will be looked down upon, probably protested, by certain entities. Some factors in this regard include government's crackdown on financial processes and dependency on the government agencies rather than the code/protocol. Before policy formulization, the governments will tackle with these challenges.

2.5   The Role of Banks

The global monetary system is complicated. It revolves around the costliest, most powerful intermediaries; we call them banks. These intermediaries regulate USD 107.5 trillion worth of global economy as of now, and draw a major portion per transaction. Bitcoin, in contrast, has something that excites up the public interest. The block-chain process of Bitcoin operates between the buyer and the seller. This open source P2P monetary system charges little-to-none fee for each transaction. This means that 1–20% of the tax fee deducted in private and commercial dealings can be saved used Bitcoin. Barclays is the world's first bank to accept Bitcoin transactions.

Bitcoin as Global Mode of Economics Via Banks

When we talk about the globalization of Bitcoin as mainstream money, we look at it at least 15-years ahead of now. In banking terms, a currency is defined with three features: limited supply, hard to earn, and easy to verify. The interest of banks in Bitcoin is vital to the interest of businesses in benefits of Bitcoin. Above all, banks have been struggling to maintain historical records and creditworthiness of their clients. Bitcoin becomes the fantasy-come-true by reflecting the client's creditworthiness and records of transactions. Bitcoin prevents double transactions using private and public addresses or key authentication system. The block-chain system provides proof of work, which reduces the chances of cyber-crime.

If we consider Mt. Gox's case here, the theft occurred due to the lack of intermediaries and authenticated policies. If banks accept Bitcoin transactions and the governments act as intermediaries, the sensitivity of Bitcoin transactions can be controlled.

Citi Report on Bitcoin as an Opportunity for the Banks

Citi Bank published a report on June 30, 2016, declaring Bitcoin as an opportunity for the banks, and not a threat. The 56-page report logically argues in the favor of digital currencies, claiming that these currencies are necessary to reach new consumers and digital global markets. Giving the example of machine-to-machine payments, the report states, '*the power behind an open network like Bitcoin is the possibility of incorporating it with other technologies to bring about true innovation, such as applications that support the Internet of Things.*'

According to the report, countries with a low-quality payment system can use open-source network like Bitcoin to improve the economic infrastructure. However, it also claims that Bitcoin is not prepared for '*prime time*'.

Integration of Bitcoin in Banking System

The banks can play a productive role in monetary management with digital currencies. Banks can use inter-bank settlements like ACH and Swift to enhance the range of Bitcoin networking. The integration will help reduce the consumer costs and transaction fees, helping the banks to expand their customer base. For consumers, the benefit of integrating Bitcoin in national and international banking system is compliance to the policies and reduction in the chances of human error.

The integration will help the banks to expand the scope of their services. People from South Pole can obtain the services of banks from the north. The use of Bitcoin will eradicate the need of local-foreign currency exchange. The cryptographic technology will assist the banks in ensuring consumer data protection and deliver the services accordingly.

The smarter way to integrate Bitcoin in banking system is to incorporate it in the infrastructure along with traditional services. The examples of such integrations are Bloomberg, The New York Times, Pandora, and iTunes.

2.6   Future Possibilities

Crypto currencies are here to stay. After the globalization of digital money, people will have a plethora of crypto-currencies for choice of use. However, some digital currencies, with high chances of Bitcoin, will have favors and support from political, economic, and industrial sector due to factors like liquidity and technological assistance. In the public sector, the most popular and largest crypto currency will be adopted by people with limited technological knowledge. At global perspective, the globalization of crypto currencies will largely follow the trends of globalization of technology. Theory of Diffusion of Innovation will stay.

Bitcoin, as a first mover and trendsetter, has self-reinforcing advantages. Bitcoin's market cap leads other crypto currencies, which means that other coins will follow the trends set by Bitcoin. It also boasts the largest global network, which refers to high liquidity and high transaction volume. Simply put, we will witness a robust mining environment, which will certainly need strengthened security.

The crypto currency ideologists will consider functional implementation of factors that will play a key role in global diffusion of these currencies. Some factors will include:

- Governments may devise policies and create rules for crypto-currencies that protect the consumers and merchants.

- Bitcoin primarily operates due to its two primary benefits: it is the currency storage and exchange medium, and it is the digital gold, that allows low-to-none fee foreign transactions. Bitcoin developers will focus on these key areas for improvements. The speed of transaction will increase. The network will expand.

- Wall Street and big businesses may embrace Bitcoin technology.

- Bitcoin may be used in international banking systems. It will replace PayPal and other online transaction resources.

- The downfall of fiat currency value will increase the value of Bitcoin.

- Bitcoin may replace money.

- Governments will issue new digital currencies.

- Block-chain technology and proof-of-work systems consume high energy resource. When the Bitcoin network grows, this may lead to increased transaction fees.

2.7 Conclusion

Traditional currency will not collapse overnight but Bitcoin will gradually takeover the building blocks of global economics. Andreas Adreano, the senior communications officer in IMF, published an article in Finance and Development Magazine. The article states that Bitcoin might have been developed to avoid conventional banks, however, the Bitcoin technology built on block-chain system is actually useful for the banks and trading systems. It says that the block-chain technology of Bitcoin is often perceived as Ponzi scheme, whereas in reality, it is the radical rewiring of financial systems.

Bitcoin, with its current deficiencies, is potent to be integrated in modern financial systems. The need of an efficient and speedy system that bodes well with instantaneous communication era and meets the requirements of the capital markets is undeniable. The key requirement lies in reaching out the new markets and consumers.

Block-chain technology has the potential of meeting private and commercial needs. In the ecommerce era, it is used as a source to purchase goods. The irrevocability of money is the only drawback, which could be legitimized and regulated for securer consumerism. The legitimization will make Bitcoin a usable mode of payments in restaurants, banks, clothing stores, and everywhere else.

Digital currencies have the potential to empower entrepreneurs and small businesses, which make up to 97% of the total corporate sky of the US. The adoption of Bitcoin by entrepreneurs can help improve the national economy at grass-root level.

Bitcoin, as a fast currency exchange method, complies with today's technological needs. The users of Bitcoin will not need to log into their bank accounts for transferring funds to the online fundraiser company. Bitcoin has the potential to initiate the transfer with one click on the 'Like' button and complete it within 10 minutes, or may be earlier in near future. Bitcoin has embraced critical mass. The time is now to accept its mass-scale popularity as financial evolution. Bitcoin may not be the primary financial resource in near future, but it will be a definite contributor of daily financial transactions.

REFERENCES

1   Ludwig, Sean (2013). Y Combinator-backed Coinbase now selling over $1M Bitcoin per month. VentureBeat. Retrieved: http://venturebeat.com/2013/02/08/coinbase-bitcoin/

2   Mandalia, Ravi (2013). The Internet Archive Starts Accepting Bitcoin Donations. Retrieved: http://web.archive.org/web/20130603175038/http://www.paritynews.com:80/web-news/item/690-the-internet-archive-starts-accepting-bitcoin-donations

3   ABC News (2013). Cypriot University to Accept Bitcoin Payments. Retrieved: http://abcnews.go.com/Technology/wireStory/cypriot-university-accept-bitcoin-payments-20962556

4   CNBC (2016). Microsoft now accepts Bitcoin to buy Xbox games and Windows apps. Retrieved: http://www.cnbc.com/2016/03/14/microsoft-stops-accepting-bitcoin-on-windows-10.html

5   ARK Investment (2015). Whitepaper: Bitcoin: A Disruptive Currency. Retrieved: http://research.ark-invest.com/bitcoin-currency

6   Japan Times (2016). Japan OKs recognizing virtual currencies as similar to real money. Retrieved: http://www.japantimes.co.jp/news/2016/03/04/business/tech/japan-oks-recognizing-virtual-currencies-similar-real-money/#.WGnhBvHythE

7   JP Nuntinx (2016). Number of Bitcoin ATMs Has More Than Doubled In Past 18 Months. Retrieved: http://themerkle.com/number-of-bitcoin-atms-has-more-than-doubled-in-past-18-months/

8   Narayanan, Arvind; Bonneau, Joseph, Felten, Edward, Miller, Andrew and Goldfeder, Steven (2016). Bitcoin and Cryptocurrency Technologies. Retrieved:

http://www.sciencedirect.com/science/article/pii/S1353485816300745

9   CoinDesk (2016). Retrieved: http://www.coindesk.com/live-blog-bitcoin-halving/

10   Cryptocompare (2016). What are Mining Rewards in Ethereum. Retrieved: https://www.cryptocompare.com/mining/guides/what-are-mining-rewards-in-ethereum/

11   Cryptocoin News (2016). XRP Price Rise Gives Ripple $500 Million Market Cap. Retrieved: https://www.cryptocoinsnews.com/xrp-price-rise-gives-ripple-500-million-market-cap/

12   The Independent (2013). Customers at Cyprus' biggest bank stung by 60% raid on savings. Retrieved: http://www.independent.co.uk/news/world/europe/customers-at-cyprus-biggest-bank-stung-by-60-raid-on-savings-8555078.html

www.ingramcontent.com/pod-product-compliance
Lightning Source LLC
Chambersburg PA
CBHW051247050326
40689CB00007B/1100